LAGUNA TALES

TALES

and

BOOMER

WAILS

A Memoir

JAMES UTT

Laguna Wails and Boomer Tales

ISBN-13: 978-1981522972

Printed in the United States of America on acid-free paper.

Typeset in Adobe Garamond Pro.

CONTENTS

Part Three: Scenes of my Laguna | 123

Part Four: Boomer Wails | 137

FOREWORD

IN 2014, A tall, handsome man walked into my Short Story Writing Workshop and sat down between two women. He immediately started charming them with his stories, and I wasn't quite sure if he had come for the company or the writing. Fortunately, he introduced himself as James Utt with the goal of writing. After teaching high school for 35 years, he was ready to focus on himself. However, short stories were not his favorite format. I enjoyed reading them, but James did not enjoy writing them. As soon as I switched him to non-fiction, he produced a new story each week.

After three sessions, James brought to class, "Alone, but Warmed by My Adopted Hometown," a beautiful essay that had us reaching for Kleenex to dab our tears.

"You could be a columnist," I said, to which he scoffed.

A few months later, I sent his essay in to the local paper and the rest is history. James became the author of the biweekly "Heart Talk" column. After he wrote over forty columns, we discussed the idea of doing a collection. Together, we went through his columns and found two universal themes: Some wailed about politics and growing old, while others relished in the wisdom gained by living seven decades. Thus, James titled the collection, *Laguna Tales and Boomer Wails.*

The beginning of the book includes stories about James before he became a columnist, most of which have never been published. They will give you insight into the man he is today: A modest, liberal retired high school teacher who grew up with an extremely famous and conservative grandfather, Congressman Utt. Context is everything, and these stories will show you a side of "Heart Talk" that you never knew.

Part Two and Part Four contain columns that he wrote for either "Heart Talk," his column in the *Laguna Beach Independent*, or for other publications.

Part Three is a beautiful collection of black and white photos that James took of his beloved Laguna Beach.

I hope that this collection will make you laugh, cry and ultimately be charmed by the way in which James expresses his views of life as a boomer who writes from the heart.

Christine Fugate

*To all the Boomers
who have a story,
but have yet to share it.*

PART ONE
THE SHAPING

GROWING UP UTT

I WAS TOLD at our family reunions that the name "Utt" was of German origin, perhaps originally spelled "Uthe" when the first of my grandfather's relatives came here from Germany, right before the Revolutionary War. My ancestors were very proud that our family predated the American Constitution. Wherever our name came from, it was unusual, if not downright odd. It rhymed with "cut," but most people pronounced it as if it rhymed with "cute." I have not heard of too many people with this last name. There were Ben Utt, who played in the NFL for eight seasons, and Kenny Utt, who was one of the producers of *Silence of the Lambs*, and before that, the classic television series *The Defenders*. Other than those two, there was James Utt, my grandfather.

From 1953 to 1961, James B. Utt was Orange County, California's only congressman. From 1961 until his death in office in 1970, he was one of only two congressmen from the county. Today, because of population growth in Southern California, there are seven members of the House that represent at least part of our county. So, in the 1950s and 1960s, this distinctive name had recognition, respect, and power in what has been termed one of the most conservative counties in the nation.

Growing up in the 1950s, whenever my name was read or spoken by someone for the first time (the beginning of school, Little League signups, Boy Scout meetings), there was almost always the question, "Are you related to Congressman Utt?" These, of course, made the preadolescent me feel very special because the people that tended to ask were generally great admirers of my grandfather.

Orange County back then, good grief, where to start. There is Lisa McGirr's excellent book, *Suburban Warriors: The Origins of the New American Right.* She tells the story, with ample references to my grandfather, of thousands of middle-class suburbanites organizing themselves into a powerful conservative movement. There were anti-communist reading groups, stop sex education groups and an explosion of evangelical churches that believed in Biblical inerrancy. I attended such churches in my youth. Well ingrained in the county's DNA was a xenophobic nationalism, a fear of the "other," be he dark skinned or Jewish. This was fertile ground for the John Birch Society, an arch conservative organization that was even denounced by William F. Buckley. They were nothing short of radical in their anti-communism and their desire for limited government. The founder, Robert Welch, even suggested President Eisenhower could have been a tool of the "communist conspiracy." They were fervently opposed to the civil rights movement because they believed there were too many communists involved in it. The popularity of this group speaks volumes about Orange County.

In the early 1960s, Orange County schools released kids from classes so they could attend Fred Swartz's "Southern California School of Anti-Communism." In the presidential election of 1964, Johnson won the state of California by garnering 60 percent of the vote. In Orange County, Goldwater got 57 percent of the vote. In 1968, *Fortune Magazine* labeled the county "nut country." This was the district that routinely returned my grandfather to Congress with 60 to 70 percent of the vote every election cycle. Ms. McGirr tells her story reflecting upon Orange County and its people, like my grandfather, from a scholarly point of view. Mine is a more personal vantage point.

As an elementary school student, I ingested, without question, the absolute fear of those my grandfather crusaded against: communists, pinkos, and fellow travelers. I learned that Jews had killed Jesus, and that the Old Testament was righteous, historically accurate, and not to be questioned. Civil rights for Negroes was a dangerous road to go down and young Martin Luther King was, very likely, a communist. In the 1960s, my grandfather received an honorary degree from Bob Jones University in South Carolina. This place of higher education, which almost every Republican candidate for president visits prior to the South Carolina primary these days, did not allow blacks to enroll until 1971. I didn't know about the restriction on enrollment or that interracial dating was forbidden. My grandfather was getting honorary degrees. Seemed pretty impressive to me, but I was too young to read the fine print.

More exciting still were the people my grandfather introduced me to while still in elementary school. Walter Knott of Knott's Berry Farm was a fellow arch conservative that I got to meet several times. One time, my grandfather arranged for me to take a ride on the Disneyland monorail with Walt Disney himself, just the two of us in the front seats. There was also Ronald Reagan, who, before he became governor, would often speak at my grandfather's campaign rallies. On a trip to Washington in sixth grade, there were introductions to Senator Goldwater and Vice President Nixon. All pretty heady stuff for a kid who was yet to sprout his first pimple.

"Why, yes, I am related to the congressman," I would proudly say in the 50s and early 60s. These were the days of hero worship. The days a picture of my grandfather shaking hands with President Eisenhower hung over my bed. He would send me excerpts of his speeches from "The Congressional Record." There were late-night interviews on television that the whole family would wait up for. There he was, my grandfather, with the power and the glory. His influence permeated the region.

The use of his name got me out of a scrape with the police. A group of my friends had committed an act of vandalism on an old house. A cop was inside waiting for the perpetrators to return to the scene of the crime and gathered us up as we approached the house. I had not engaged in the destruction at the home, had not even known about it. As the policeman began to question us, I mentioned how disappointed my grandfather, the congressman, would be that his grandson was suspected of such an act. The cop immediately let me be on my way, but kept the other boys for further questioning,

No discussion of my childhood would be complete without mentioning my father. He was immature, weak, and hurtful. My grandfather knew that his only child would never scale to great heights. I think that my father knew this, too. The only success he had came by virtue of his last name. One time in Las Vegas, he was drunk and bragged about whom his father was. He threatened the casino workers that they better "treat him right." They took him to the city limits and dumped him in the desert. He was lucky the mob didn't do worse.

There may have been some goodness, some decency in my father, but these qualities were easily overshadowed by a legion of despicable characteristics. He was a drunk whose drinking buddies would dump him in our front yard. My mother and I would do our best to get this 230-pound man into the house. Once we were out to eat at a nice restaurant and he passed out, face-first into his mashed potatoes. Coming to, he told the waitress, "I want blue cheese on my salad."

He was cruel to my sisters. One time, he put my younger sister in the trunk of his car and drove around for a while to teach her to not talk back to him. He made fun of my other sister's weight. But, he was most cruel to my mother. He cheated, cheated, and cheated again on her. One of his girlfriends actually called our house to tell my mother he was staying the night with her. The husband of one of his women came looking for my dad at the beverage company my grandfather had bought for him. The husband had a gun. The only reason my dad escaped from harm was thanks to the quick thinking of a coworker. Ours was not a "Father Knows Best" home.

My dad was a virulent racist. Terms like "wetback," "chink," "coon," "nigger," and "kike" echoed off the walls of our house. Perhaps his bigotry came from the fact that he was an uneducated man. He dropped out of high school when my mother became pregnant. The congressman never used such terms and would correct his son when he used racial epithets around me. His bigotry was cloaked in more scholarly words. He was a gentleman congressman, not Strom Thurmond who used racial slurs at will.

Once, when my grandfather was over for dinner and I wanted to show him how ignorant my father was and how smart his grandson was, I asked, "So, dad, when did the colonies declare their independence from England?"

He tried to laugh off the question, but his father made him answer. "1876," he stammered.

Indeed, it would not be my father, but me whom my grandfather would groom for excellence. As a congressman, he had the power to appoint me to one of the military academies and hoped that someday I would wear an officer's uniform. Another soldier for God and country.

From junior high school through the first three years of high school, my ultra-conservatism was my shield, my identity. *I* had a famous grandfather. *I* had met important people. *I* knew the real danger of the communist menace. In class when assignments or discussions took a political turn, mine was always the far right stance.

There was one debate, I can't even remember the topic, where I faced off against, oh dear lord, an actual liberal Democrat, and a very smart one at that. To the best of my knowledge he easily won our debate and ended his statement with, "Unfortunately, there will always be people like Jim Utt." Shaken and mad, I returned to my seat. No one had ever challenged me before. No one had ever challenged my grandfather's views to my face before.

It did not happen like a Saul on the road to Damascus moment. It was more a gradual questioning which led to a crumbling of the political ground upon which my grandfather had placed me. In 1963, when I was a sophomore, CBS did an hour long special entitled, "Case History of a Rumor," narrated by Roger Mudd. In those days, our televisions with antennas on our roofs got about six or seven stations. Because there were so few, each had a large viewing audience. In this hour-long devastation of my grandfather, Mudd reported that Mr. Utt claimed "a large contingent of barefoot Africans" might be training in Georgia as part of a United Nations military exercise to take over the United States. I knew my grandfather hated the UN and introduced a bill each session of Congress to have the United States withdraw from this organization. But this? Yikes. No use of "coon" or the "n word," but "barefoot Africans" sent a pretty clear racial stereotype. And the whole idea seemed, well, loony, even to me.

Tustin High School was filled with students who parroted their parents' conservative views, but the next day, kids I didn't even know came up and asked, "Are you related to that guy on TV last night?"

"Yeah," I would answer, and walk quickly away. My grandfather sued CBS for defamation of character and lost.

I began to wonder, for the first time, if my grandfather was a bit too extreme, too much on the fringe. I began to wonder about his whole philosophy. It was like the *Titanic* hitting the iceberg, a slow but steady leak that would sink our relationship.

But, even after the CBS special, Orange County was still "Utt Country," and he kept racking up huge electoral victories. The general view was liberal CBS had done a "hit piece" on the gentleman congressman. No lasting harm. But the more I learned about his voting record, and the more tough questions were posed to me in class, especially by that rarest of creatures, a liberal teacher in Tustin, the more uncomfortable I became with defending the congressman's positions.

Shortly after the CBS program, I learned that my grandfather had helped author a minority report in the House that advised to vote against admitting Hawaii to the United States. Part of the reason for his position was that Hawaii had "an atmosphere of tolerance, appeasement, and encouragement for communism." I overheard from family discussions that he was also very concerned that there were too many nonwhites and not enough Christians in this archipelago. After all, America was meant to be white and Protestant.

In 1963 and 1964, I witnessed on our scratchy black-and-white television how Negroes were treated in the South as they marched for basic civil rights. Sheriff "Bull" Connor, police dogs, fire hoses, jeers by racist thugs. Who could not be moved by such scenes? Yet my grandfather voted against the 1964 Civil Rights Bill that would outlaw discriminations on the basis of race in public accommodations.

"We have to protect property rights." Nothing was mentioned about human rights.

There was the March on Washington, where Martin Luther King gave his stirring "I Have a Dream" speech. The only thing I remember my grandfather mentioning from this historical event was that the marchers left a lot of trash behind. There were also rumors of interracial sex, a subject of great concern to him, and to most who lived in Orange County at the time.

In 1965, the nation saw the violence that occurred at the Edmund Pettus Bridge on "Bloody Sunday," as peaceful marchers, supporting the right for black people to vote, were set upon in a most violent fashion by the police. Yet, the congressman voted against the 1965 Voting Rights Bill.

"Too much federal interference in the business that should properly fall to the states," was his reason.

By the mid-sixties, the Beatles had arrived and rock music was making a large impact on youth culture. My grandfather considered rock and roll, along with anything that smacked of pornography, of being an effort by the communists to weaken the fiber of American youth. This seemed pretty damned silly. In fact, I was the first student to wear a Beatle wig to school. It was quickly confiscated by the vice principal.

By the time of my graduation from high school, I had taken one firm step away from the arch conservative views that prevailed in

Orange County: I had decided that the death penalty was wrong. Of course, I kept this view from my grandfather who would have considered it a betrayal of the rock-solid teachings of the Old Testament. But my tentative steps away from the John Birch philosophy would soon be followed by leaps and bounds toward a worldview that offered more reason and humanity.

In 1965, I was in the first class to open the University of California at Irvine. The day before classes began, a trip to the bookstore was in order. I remember one text had the outrageous price of $11. Passing by the magazine section, a friend pointed out one particular publication whose cover story was entitled, "Mr. Utt's War With the 20th Century." I chose not to buy a copy, knowing pretty well what would be inside. In my new surroundings, the question, "Are you related to Congressman Utt?" took on a whole new meaning. I lasted only two years at UCI before the rigorous math requirements for social science majors forced me to find a less demanding school. But before my time as an "Anteater" ended, I did something that would hasten the explosion that occurred between my grandfather and me.

The dominant newspaper at the time was the *Register*, whose editorial page made the *Wall Street Journal's* editorial page look like that of the *Nation*. All forms of public education were considered socialistic. I wrote a letter to the editor praising UCI, defending public education in general, and questioning the wisdom of those who thought otherwise. Of course, they attached an "Editor's Note" to my letter explaining the 'true' definition of socialism and how misguided public education had made me. But there it was, a moderately liberal letter written by James E. Utt. Oh, no. There would be reverberations; an Utt who had taken a non-conservative position.

The next time I saw my grandfather, he told me that he could no longer financially support my college education because my views where so divergent from his. By this time, my mother had divorced my father due to his flagrant infidelity and money was in short supply. She could have gone after my father on grounds of adultery, but was pressured by my grandfather to file under grounds of "irreconcilable differences." Adultery would have been too embarrassing for all he told her, meaning himself more than anyone else. My mother also told me that the solidly religious man, who wanted to make Christianity the national religion of the USA, told her, "Often a man needs more than one woman." How many religious right hypocrites have been uncovered over the years? The righteous governor of Alabama comes immediately to mind.

The Vietnam War raged with increasing intensity as the 60s moved on and the draft loomed for me after graduation from college. I was, of course by this time, an opponent, while my grandfather saw it as a life-and-death struggle between the free world and communism. His position was similar to General Curtis LeMay, who was George Wallace's running mate in 1968 for the American Independent Party. "We should bomb them back to the Stone Age." I, on the other hand, was listening to Country Joe and the Fish's "I-Feel-Like-I'm-Fixin'-to-Die Rag."

No statehood for Hawaii, no civil rights for blacks, no sex education because it was a communist plot, the United Nations a distinct threat to the USA, support of a war that poured more and more Americans into the meat grinder that was Vietnam, a war I believed was only causing misery for all, especially the Vietnamese—how could any rational, compassionate person hold these views? With an anger that often only youth can possess, I came to detest my grandfather's positions, beliefs, and values. To hide my changes would be a betrayal of myself. I made no secret of the fact that I had begun to attend a Unitarian church. It was Unitarians who offered sanctuary to military deserters, and their doctrines were a far cry from the fundamentalist churches of my younger days.

Learning this fact about me was a severe blow to my grandfather, who was becoming more and more aware of the metamorphosis that was taking place in the grandson who he had wanted to go to West Point.

Although he had cut me off financially, we still had contact on occasion. For some reason that was lost in the maelstrom that was to come, I went over to his house, and the inevitable political discussion began, which was actually started by my grandmother, who was as conservative as he. This was no James Carville, Mary Matalin marriage. I was hit by questions, my answers only provoking more angry questions. Finally, she asked, "Would you even vote for your grandfather?"

I could have lied and said yes. Maybe I should have voted for him because he was my kin. But no. My anti-war, pro civil rights, Bobby Kennedy for president temperament would not allow me to say anything, but, "No, I don't think so."

My grandfather, who had been quiet up to this point of the conversation, looked at me coldly and said, "I would rather see you dead and buried in Vietnam than think the way you do now."

And so the journey that began with prideful hero worship, rides with Walt Disney, and being treated preferentially because of my last name had come to an end. With a jolt, a painful, hateful jolt.

I should mention at this point my maternal grandmother, who, believe it or not, was even more conservative than my grandfather. She had the *Blue Book of the John Birch Society* on her nightstand. Instead of wishing me dead, she continued to have me over for dinner each Sunday and joked about my (she hoped) temporary leftist views. "If you were an Indian, your name would be Charlie Left Foot," she said and went on loving me until the day she died. Thank you, Nana Hellen.

The congressman's health began to decline around this time. Members of his side of the family put much of the blame on me. "What a betrayal he must have felt when his own grandson turned against him!" "How could he be so ungrateful?" "You know how a broken heart can weaken your health." One great aunt came over to our house and screamed at my mother for letting me become a kook, pinko, a dupe of the Communist party, a traitor to the family. "How could your son stab a man in the back who was fighting so hard to defend our freedoms?" Finally, she screamed herself out and left. Fortunately, I had been in the bathroom and did not come out until her car pulled out of the driveway. I was now an Utt in name only to my father's side of the family.

Congressman James B. Utt died in 1970, still in office, serving his constituents, the majority of who felt he was doing a fine job for the people of Orange County. Again, his death brought claims from the family that his demise was, at least in part, due to his traitorous grandson, who had broken his heart and his spirit. Why, they whispered, the kid probably smoked pot (I did), and engaged in premarital sex (I had). Little consideration was given to the fact that the congressman was 70 and had been a heavy smoker over the years.

I tried my best, my very best, not to carry his death on my conscience. Most of the time, I was successful in doing this, but not always. If there was such a thing as a "generation gap," in the 1960s, it applied to the two of us. The immovable object of white privilege and fear of "the other," meeting the raging, idealistic, sometimes too impetuous spirit of youth. In my case it was an unfortunate collision, but an inevitable one.

I did attend my grandfather's funeral, which was held at the Crystal Cathedral, at that time presided over by the famous Rev. Schuller. Now, Governor Reagan was there and was very gracious to my sisters and me. After the service a large procession of cars snaked its way to the cemetery. I was in a limo with one of my grandfather's senior aides. We noticed that the police had closed the freeway to all traffic but ours. The aide looked out the window and said, "How nice and respectful this is. I wouldn't even mind if they did this for a Negro funeral."

My father got his father's desk from his office in Washington and gathered other artifacts from his time in office and created a type of shrine in a spare bedroom in his new wife's home. It was his way of honoring a father he had let down. In the rare occasions I visited my father, I only went in that room once. Trying to put his memory behind me was easier said than done. Who he was, the things he stood for, the words he had said to me, left deep wounds that were bandaged but did not heal. There is a line from The Band that says,

"He may forgive, or he may regret, but he will never, ever, forget." I haven't. This, coupled with my father's weaknesses, has left me with issues of inadequacy and angst that I deal with today at age 68. I have tried with all my heart to raise my two sons in such a way as to avoid the small-mindedness and paranoia of my grandfather and the cruelty and ignorance of my father. I wanted their experience of growing up Utt to be so different from my own. They are in their thirties now and tell me they are proud of me.

This is a balm for my heart.

FAT TUESDAY

My mother had me when she was a sophomore in high school. "Roe v. Wade" was decades away, so she had no other choice but to marry my father. His parents blamed my mother for luring their son with the famous name into a sexual relationship so she could escape her family's poverty.

Her "family" was just she and her mother, her father having disappeared right after my mother was born, never to be heard from again. She and her mother slept together in a bed that pulled down from the wall that took up most of the "living room" when it was in use. Money and food were in short supply and my grandmother would often leave my mother with her sister, my great aunt, as she went to different parts of the state to pick fruit, the only occupation she had ever known.

Yes, my mother was poor. She was often hungry, I am sure. But I am also sure she would never use sex at age 15 to escape her plight. Based on my father's behavior as a man, or rather, man-child, it was he who took advantage of a vulnerable young girl. His parents quite probably believed this in their heart of hearts, but could never bring themselves to admit it.

In the late 1940s, and early 1950s, it was seen as the wife's job to foster a happy home. If something went awry, the woman was often blamed for not creating the proper home environment. Think of *Leave it to Beaver* to prove the point. Mrs. Cleaver would be doing housework, vacuuming, or cooking, and when Ward came home from a full day of doing whatever he did, a wonderfully prepared dinner was soon at hand. But our family was not the Cleavers, and certainly not "Father Knows Best." "Father Acts Worst" would have been a more apt title. Philandering, drinking, and lying do not a happy home environment make. Confronted with my father's flagrant infidelity, my mother could stand no more. Had I been older, I would have learned about the time a husband of one of my father's girlfriends came after him with a gun. I would have been more aware of his drunkenness, lying, and cruel treatment toward my mother and sisters, including the time I mentioned in which he locked one of them in the trunk of his car as he drove her home from a friend's where she had stayed too long. I, as "the son," escaped most of his cruelty, as if I was being trained to inherit his behavior.

In the late 1950s, my mother filed for divorce. She told me years later, "I could have gone after him for adultery, but your grandfather scared me into settling on grounds of 'irreconcilable differences.'" My father's father was the most well known politician in our county, and it would have been embarrassing to have his son's name splashed across the pages of the local paper as an adulterer. This powerful man, who would fit well into today's evangelical Tea Party mold, told my mother, "A man often needs more than one woman."

So, my father emerged financially undamaged, and with most of his name intact. My mother got to keep the house, but received very little alimony and child support. My father did his best to prove his father's axiom that a man needed more than one woman. Two marriages and several affairs followed. It would be difficult to determine which one of his three ex-wives hated him more.

My mother faced a daunting future. She was a high school dropout with three kids and no job or skills other than "homemaking," as it was called back then. We lived in a neighborhood that did not know the real story of the breakup. Consequently, many on our street looked upon her with a degree of suspicion or outright scorn. She had driven the Congressman's son away; she had not provided the proper home life that could keep a family together.

What little money she received was quickly gobbled up by the necessities of running the household. Mortgage payments, car repairs, clothes from J.C. Penney, doctor bills, and, of course, food. We did need to eat. My dear maternal grandmother went back to work at a packinghouse. Those were the days when Orange County actually had oranges. She stood on varicose veins, grading oranges so she could supplement my mother's meager supply of cash. On Sundays, we would pile into our 1951 Chevy and go to her house for dinner that always consisted of the driest roast ever prepared on the North American continent. But it was made for us by loving hands, and with enough gravy and creamed corn, it could be, well, palatable.

This kind person also gave her daughter money so she could attend the Sawyer School of Business in Santa Ana and acquire enough skills to find a job outside the home. Now, we needed a babysitter, especially for my young sisters. Enter Gertrude, an old gal who knew the real story of my father's unfaithfulness and agreed to watch us during the day for very little money. All she asked for in return was that she be allowed to bring over a case of Rainier Ale and have control of the television for certain hours.

After a day of downing her Rainier Ale, Gertrude whipped up concoctions that might be considered "enhanced interrogation techniques" should the inmates at Gitmo be forced to consume them. I remember a terribly watery potato soup. There was also something called "tamale pie." Dinners were often vegetables and rice. The only trouble was that I hated green vegetables. Perhaps this stemmed from my younger years when my father would force open my mouth and ram broccoli down my throat.

I longed for the infrequent hamburger patty, or that greatest of all God's creations, the TV dinner.

My mother had a chance to escape our poverty during the time she was in the business school, but it would come at a price. There was a man, I believe his name was John Jones, who had done business with my father and had met my mother on occasions. He asked my mother out for dinner. When he came to the door, the first and only thing I noticed about him was his age. Ten or eleven at the time, probably everyone over thirty looked old to me, but I thought he looked like Walter Brennan in the series *The Real McCoys*, just a lot better dressed. I learned from my mother he had money, lots of it. The second time he asked her out I was also invited and what a date it was. October 1959, game three of the first World Series played in Los Angeles. John got us seats directly behind home plate. I saw Duke Snider, Carl Furillo, and Don Drysdale up close. I ate hot dogs, chips, sodas, and candy. I felt like a conquering Viking that had just plundered the food stores of some defenseless village. The Dodgers won, by the way.

On the way out of the stadium, I saw John put his arm around my mother.

I did not miss my father, but this was a very awkward sight for me to see. Grandpa with his arm around my mother. She had a decision to make, be with a man, a much older man, and have no more worries about feeding her family again, or be true to her feelings and stay in poverty. She would not marry a man she did not love and I never saw John Jones again.

Speaking of hot dogs, Fridays were hot dog day at my elementary school. Schools providing hot dogs for young growing bodies? Remember these were the 1950s when cigarettes were still advertised on television; hot dogs were seen as practically a health food back then. Right after the divorce, my mother could not afford even the modest price for these lunches. So, every Friday, I ate what was in my Davy Crockett lunch pail, instead of the mouth-watering hot dogs dripping with mustard and ketchup. There usually wasn't much in old Davy, so I ate slowly, not wanting to bring attention to this fact. If I knew enough about the Catholic faith back then, I could have told my classmates that the reason I never had Hostess Sno Balls or Twinkies was because being a Catholic—which of course I was not—my mother had forced me to give up sweets for Lent. But that also would have come at a price, since Orange County was a virtual WASP hive back then and I would have been seen not only as the poor kid, but also the one who followed an idol-worshipping religion.

Perhaps because I was the oldest, or the family member most in need of spiritual guidance, my mother saw fit to give in to my great aunt and uncle's suggestion that I spend frequent weekends with them. They were very religious and, unbeknownst to me at the time, very wealthy. But in true Calvinist tradition, they never showed an outward display of such earthly success. Food was never an issue when I stayed with them. They grew their own boysenberries that I put on top of my shredded wheat. There were tasty tuna and chopped celery sandwiches for lunch. For dinner, we usually walked, rather than take the old Studebaker, to a cafeteria down the street. I picked the fish sticks because I could slather them with tartar sauce. But, I also had to eat vegetables. If I tried to hide them, I was told there would be no dessert at home and was reminded, "There are children starving in India."

After Saturday's bounty of boysenberries and cafeteria food came the required church service. They attended a strict evangelical church, and being hungry for structure and guidance, I devoured the teachings as would anyone convinced of their sinfulness. I ignored the inherent cruelty and contradictions of the Bible until my college years, when I came to accept agnosticism as readily as a child accepts a freshly baked cookie on a cool autumn afternoon.

My bedroom at home was close to the kitchen and late into the night, I could hear my mother practicing typing on an ancient typewriter. She worked on homework from the business school long after I fell asleep, yet got up the next morning with a smile and fixed us as good a breakfast as much as our meager budget would allow.

Going to restaurants was a rare occurrence. However one day, my mother took us to Knott's Berry Farm for their specialty, fried chicken made from Mrs. Knott's secret recipe. Oh, what a feast this was! I even ate my vegetables, because I could mix them with the mound of mashed potatoes that came with the chicken. These were the days before Knott's was an amusement park. Just down the freeway was the relatively new wonder world of Disneyland, which was completely out of our price range. I had to content myself by hearing stories of classmates' visits, adding that my family was going there very soon.

Other images from this time still linger in my mind: My sisters getting thinner, being at the dentist with my stomach growling loudly, and my mother skipping meals so we could eat. But these are not the images that dominate my memories of those years. I have the image of a one-parent family that had it tough, but made it. The Beatles might have oversimplified it a bit when they sang, "All you need is love," but they essentially got it right. There are more sustaining things than calories. We had our mother's love, her undying efforts to hold us together. It was enough.

All her late-night studying and typing paid off and she graduated from business school with high marks. She soon landed her first job, as, of course, a secretary. The day she got her first paycheck, she brought home steaks, which my sisters and I looked upon as one might look upon creatures thought to be extinct. She baked potatoes and for my benefit, also substituted the usual green vegetables with creamed corn. It was a Tuesday, which I will forever remember as our "Fat Tuesday."

Food was never an issue again. She had beaten the odds and shown my father's side of the family she would not be broken. That after the divorce, the girl from the wrong side of the tracks had the moral fiber that her ex-husband lacked. There were times after the divorce when there was not enough food in our house, but we never went hungry for the things that mattered.

I am at her gravesite this day looking down on the plaque that marks where her ashes are buried. It is next to her mother and one of my sisters. I do not know where she is, if she "is," or whether or not there is a chance she can read my mind. In the slim chance that she can, I whisper a soft "thank you."

THE GRENADE RANGE

It did not look like the hand grenades I had seen actors throw in the hundreds of war movies I had watched before 1970. It was smaller, more round, but it did have the circular "pin" protruding from its little body that when pulled would make it explode in five seconds. A grizzled sergeant was about to hand me my first live grenade, which I was to throw at the pile of tires many yards away.

Until it was our turn to trot down to the throwing area, we were kept far away. We could still hear the earsplitting explosions, smell the distinctive odor of the exploding tires, and whatever agent was packed inside the little bombs. Half of our company was acting like what they were about to do was the most exciting thing since loosening that first bra strap in high school. The other half was quiet, trying not to show their fear. I was scared shitless.

We had all heard the story. Last week a recruit froze after he pulled the pin and held on to the grenade too long. He blew his head off and killed the instructor next to him. Images of brain and blood splashed on the concrete barrier would not leave my mind. This was not like the old World War II films where people got shot and even killed by a grenade, yet did not bleed.

It was my turn. We went three at a time to concrete structures that had three sides. The walls were about four feet high. There were deep ditches along the inside of the structures where the instructor could kick a dropped grenade and then fall on top of the recruit before it exploded. This has got to be the worst job in the Army. I was never afraid on the rifle range and was actually an excellent shot. I killed many Viet Cong paper targets. But my rifle could not turn around and shoot me. If a grenade is handled incorrectly, you died or were maimed for life.

"You're going to pull the pin exactly when I tell you. You are going to then quickly put it slightly behind your ear like you're gonna throw a pass. Then when I say throw, you let that grenade fly toward those tires and duck your ass down."

I was about to throw a bomb. If held on to for too long, I die. If dropped, the sergeant has to kick it down the safety hole. I will be ridiculed or worse. Guts tightened, bowels felt like they might let go.

"Pull!"

This fucking thing was next to my head. How many seconds? Is he waiting too long? Tell me to throw it, throw it. I don't want to kill us both. I almost throw it before he gives the command.

"Throw!"

Relief flooded through my body. I had done it. It was over.

"What the fuck was that? My five-year-old girl could throw it farther than you just did. You gotta do better than that soldier! Now for your second throw I want to see you strap on some balls and throw it a hell of a lot farther."

Oh, Christ. That's right, we had to toss two grenades. I could hear the other instructors complimenting the two that had just thrown their grenades.

Not only had my first throw been inadequate, I had pissed off my instructor. Once again, the pin would be pulled and the little ball of death, thrown so easily in war movies, would be next to my head. This time with more pressure. Thoughts danced through my mind. Performance anxiety, self-fulfilling prophesies, the headless draftee.

"Dear Mrs. Utt, We regret to inform you that your son James was killed in a training exercise. He was an inept pussy."

As I waited for the second grenade to be handed to me, the strangest memory came into my mind. The first time I tried to have sex with Pam Thomas was about as successful as my first throw. But the second time, after a few beers, we fucked until we sweated. Trembling fear was replaced by anger and resolve as I pulled the pin.

"This one's for you, Pam. See how far I can fuck, I mean throw," I said to myself as I flung the grenade. I suddenly understood why some men get erections during battle.

"Well, that's a lot better, soldier. There's hope for you yet."

I never threw another grenade, and Pam Thomas never responded to any of my letters.

MAGNETIC NORTH

PEOPLE SEARCH FOR something that will give meaning to their lives, something that will serve as an anchor that will keep them from drifting to the waters of despair or meaninglessness. For so many, especially in the United States, this anchor is religion. I know how comforting this anchor can be, also how restricting.

Raised in an evangelical household in Tustin in the 1950s, we had it instilled in us that the Bible was inerrant and that the god of the Old Testament was tough, but righteous. Jews had killed Jesus, and unless you were "born again," you would be condemned to hell's hot fires for eternity. Christianity was the only hope for sinful mankind, as well as the only defense against godless communism. These were not uncommon views in Orange County at the time.

My grandfather Congressman James B. Utt reinforced these views. He saw the United Nations as a godless force that was bent on world domination. He very much wanted Christianity to be declared the national religion of the United States. As a boy, I drank in these beliefs as a thirsty man drinks water after a long day's work. Such was the depth of my fundamentalist beliefs that when I saw the movie *Inherit the Wind*, about the Scopes trial, I actually felt the character representing William Jennings Bryan got the better of the Clarence

Darrow character. "Onward Christian Soldiers" was my favorite song growing up as a preteen.

As one grows up, it seems they either cling more tightly to the beliefs of their youth or begin a questioning, a rebellion. The 1960s arrived and I took the latter course. Probing college professors and wider experiences led me to reflect more deeply on my earlier religious beliefs. Biblical inerrancy, the brutality of the god of the Old Testament, the concept of hell, these beliefs and others fell away as quickly as leaves departing a tree in late autumn.

In the late 1960s, I discovered a Unitarian church in Santa Ana and began to attend regularly.

The Unitarians were taking a stand against the Vietnam War and other social injustices. There was a belief in the divine, but it was a far cry from the deity that ordered the slaughter of so many innocents, and condemned nonbelievers to hell. My heart and, I thought, my soul soared in these few months that I shared Sunday mornings with my fellow believers. I believed I had found my true north.

In 1970, Congressman Utt died and thousands of Bible-believing Christians turned out for his funeral at the Crystal Cathedral, as well as one Bible-doubting Unitarian. As I walked into the main hall, it struck me that this church of glass and fountains was a far cry from what a carpenter from Galilee would want erected in his honor.

About this time, I drew an unlucky number in the draft lottery. More fortunate than most draftees, my destination was not South Vietnam, but South Korea, to be part of a deterrent force to keep North Korea in check. There, amid a haze of marijuana smoke, liquor, and inexpensive prostitutes, we helped defend the repressive and authoritarian regime of President Park in this "outpost of freedom."

This was a time of disillusionment and loneliness. There was no Unitarian church to inspire and support me. Returning home, religion was now in my rearview mirror. Sundays were for watching football or nursing a hangover. It was the 1970s, and the Orange County mega churches like Calvary Chapel in Costa Mesa were becoming very popular. Many people my age were drawn to them, including former hippies looking for a new type of drug, one I had no taste for.

Shortly after my discharge, Kathy entered my life. She was a good woman, better than I deserved. We soon married and started a family. As a new father, I wondered if our boys needed a structured belief system. My own secular humanism suddenly seemed too thin a broth to give my life full meaning.

Could one be good without God? Was there the possibility of a transcendent reality? Old questions began to poke through the wreckage of my broken faith. Someone gave me a book by the radical Catholic theologian Hans Kung. It was compelling. I searched out books by other liberal Catholics and came to the conclusion that one could be both a Christian and a man of reason without taking Kierkegaard's "leap of faith." I became a joyous Catholic, a Catholic of Vatican II, a Catholic who fought for social justice.

So began nearly 20 years of Saturday evening mass—still had to have Sundays free to watch the Steelers, regular confessions, and prayer before dinner. My wife taught religious education classes and I even became a Notre Dame football fan. Once again, I thought I had found my true north.

MY REAL TRUE NORTH

My years as a contented Catholic came and went. The waters of doubt and disbelief slowly rose and covered the rock that was my faith.

A friend offered an explanation for my becoming a nonbeliever. Since my grandfather (the congressman and ultimate authority figure in my youth) said he wished me dead when he learned I could not support him for reelection, my rebellion against God was merely a belated rebellion against him. If she is right, I could end this essay right now, but I do not think she is.

More likely is the realization I was a "cafeteria Christian" who picked the parts of the faith that were beautiful and moving and ignored the rest. If Christians read the entire Bible carefully, many would come to agree with Richard Dawkins that "the God of the Old Testament is arguably the most unpleasant character in all of fiction." Petty, unjust, genocidal, misogynistic—these are a few of the things that come to mind when thinking about the being that supposedly created the universe in six days. Here is but one example of so many I could give that shook my faith. It comes from 1 Sam. 15:3, where the lord God orders his chosen people to destroy the Amalekites. "…Do not spare them; put to death men and woman, children and infants."

How can one believe in, let alone worship a god that orders the death of infants? I'm talking to you, jealous pro-life Christians.

Then there is the idea of Hell. Is Gandhi in hell, Jonas Salk, Thomas Jefferson? None believed Jesus was the messiah, none were born again. They get the same punishment as Hitler and this is supposed to be just?

My wife contracted cancer in 1999. Thus began a 14-year battle that would take one breast, then the other. The disease could not be stopped and spread to her liver. Painful treatments and procedures, hour after hour of chemo could not stem the tide. She fought so bravely. Hairless, courageous, defiant, hopeful, and finally resigned, she died in 2013. On her last night, we heard no angels singing and saw no approaching light as I injected more and more morphine into her ravaged body. There were only the mournful cries of pain that stay with me unto this day. If God is all-powerful, why does he let his creations suffer so? There is the theory that God sends suffering to test our faith. What type of God would do such a thing? I guess the same one that told Abraham to murder his son as an act of faith.

In 2012, my mother died. My sisters, who still believed in god and the afterlife, and I felt an acute sense of loss. My younger sister, the most emotionally fragile among us, was also burdened by ailments that legions of doctors were unable to address. Shortly before Thanksgiving, we attended the funeral of a cousin who had fought, like so many, a losing battle with cancer. The minister, trying to soothe the broken hearts said, "Her suffering is over. She is now with her loved ones in heaven."

I should have been aware as to how this message would affect my sister. The day after Thanksgiving she told her husband, "I miss mom so much. I wish I could see her again." When he returned from surfing that day, he found her hanging from a rope in the garage, a Bible at her feet. At barely 100 pounds, this was no quick death, but an agonizing strangling, with limbs kicking as a slow choking drained the life from her.

My sister's ashes are buried next to my mother's. Both urns are in the same plot as my maternal grandmother's casket. Visiting this site where three dearly loved relatives lay, I was approached by two men who tried to give me literature about their brand of Christianity. What an intrusion, what a crossing of boundaries, what lack of common decency.

There may be a God, but I agree with the late Vincent Bugliosi, who said in his book *Divinity of Doubt*, it is certainly not the God of the Middle Eastern religions.

After all these years, I know who and what I am. I am an agnostic. I cannot be an atheist. That just seems like another form of fundamentalism. All the stops I made along the way, Protestant fundamentalism, Unitarianism, Catholicism, Jeffersonian Deism, were alluring but deceptive magnetic norths. One can be good without God. I have, after all these years, found my true north.

Someone asked me if it was easier being a nonbeliever. "No," I replied, "not easier, just truer."

I wished my sister could have lived with this truth.

PART TWO
LAGUNA TALES

IF YOU CAN KEEP YOUR HEAD

MY FRIEND RECENTLY said, "Jim, your columns are too serious, dealing with personal loss and societal problems. You need to lighten up." Then, my tennis partner said, "You make snide comments about Newport Beach so often they just might take it too personally and launch an armada of their yachts against our undefended coastline." Okay, fine! You want a comedy, a farce? Let me tell you about the time my cat almost caused my death.

Jack the Cat is old and has diabetes, which means two shots a day and a special diet. As a consequence of his illness, he drinks massive amounts of water, which, because we spoiled him, he will only take from faucets. He is so obsessed with water that when I am in the shower, he stands on his back legs and paws the glass with his front legs. At the first light of day, he paws my face, as I lay asleep, telling me, "Hey, it's morning. Turn on the faucet."

We got Jack in 2002 from the shelter in the canyon where he and his tiny five brothers and sisters had been left in a cardboard box late one night. When they were old enough to be adopted, my wife and I asked for "the most spirited" of the litter. Jack proved to be that and more. Since we had door handles instead of doorknobs, Jack soon learned he could jump up, hang on to a handle, and swing any door open. He could also, and this is something I should have paid more attention to, stand on his back legs, put his front paws on a drawer, walk backwards and open it. Why he did this I do not know. The drawer he opened most frequently was in the guest bathroom and contained Q-tips, soap, and Preparation H. Why he needed any of those, I am not sure.

One very hot day, he followed me into the guest bathroom and bellowed loudly, as he so often does, for water. "Hey, it's hot, I've got fur, and have diabetes. Stop what you are doing and turn on the damn faucet." I think that was a loose translation. Wanting a moment's peace, I flung him from the inner bathroom and shut the door. A moment later, I tried to open the door and found it would not open. The drawer with the Preparation H was blocking it. Jack had trapped me in my own bathroom.

How would I ever escape? My wife having passed and my sons in different cities, I was alone. I tried to muscle the door enough to break the drawer, but found a dramatic lack of muscles for this task. There is a small window, not big enough to crawl through, that faces the street. I could call for help. Not that many people walk along my street and after an hour I had seen no one. I began to ask myself, how would it sound to a perfect stranger if I called out, "Hey! I am trapped in my own bathroom. Yeah, by my cat. If I tell you where I hide my extra key would you come in and set me free?" For all they knew, I could be Hannibal Lector waiting with a nice bottle of Chianti.

Yes, I would die in my own bathroom, trapped by my cat. I was already getting hungry. At least I had the shower, so I would die clean. Eventually my body would be found, and CSI Laguna would dust for prints and discover evidence of Jack's involvement. I hoped he would be charged with first-degree murder, but some smarty-pants PETA lawyer would probably get it reduced to reckless endangerment.

Then for some reason the first line of a Rudyard Kipling poem popped into my head, "If you can keep your head, while all those around you are losing theirs." That's all I could remember. I had, as is often the case, not kept my head, but lost it when the initial panic of being trapped set in. It suddenly dawned on me that I would not die a clean and lonely death. I had a cell phone in my pocket. A call to my neighbor, and I was free. He was gracious enough not to laugh, or ask why a man who lives alone needs to shut the door to the bathroom when he is in it.

Jack eventually emerged from hiding. He looked at me and said, "Now do you understand whom you are dealing with?"

James Utt is a retired social science teacher who has lived in Laguna since 2001. He often loses his head.

THANKSGIVING WITH
TWO STUDENTS

When I was young and healthy, the only doctor I came in contact with was Doc Martens and his classic work boots, which I wore when I was trying to affect a rugged look. Now that I am three score and eight, I seem to have more doctors and therapists than friends. Let's see, there are the internist, the cardiologist, the gastroenterologist, the neurologist, the orthopedic guys, and all the rehab workers that try their best to keep me on the court. Of course, my weakening eyesight requires an optometrist, who recently recommended that I see an ophthalmologist to have my retinas checked.

So, a couple of days before Thanksgiving, I found myself in the examination room, palms sweaty, wondering if I would have a detached retina like Sugar Ray Leonard had years ago. But since I was not a professional boxer, I knew the chances of that were slim, yet still. The doctor entered the room and I extended a hand I hoped was not too wet and said how nice it was to meet him.

"Actually, Mr. Utt, we have met before. I was a student in your honors Cultural Geography class at El Toro High School."

Amazingly, I did recognize him, then the hard working "A" student, now a noted eye specialist from Princeton. He told me he still remembered lessons that we did and how valuable they were. He did not remember many of the El Toro staff, but he remembered me, and gave heartfelt thanks for being someone who had inspired him.

Half an hour later, having learned that my retinas were fine, eyes still recovering from the dilation, the street looking a "whiter shade of pale" even with dark glasses on, I felt damn good. I had learned I had made an impact on a student who was now a huge success. That is why I got into teaching. That is why all good teachers get into teaching. Over the years, other former students had written me letters, thanking me for what I had helped them learn and discover about themselves. I keep them all in a suitcase that would be the first thing I grab in case of a fire. Hey, I live in Mystic Hills where we always sweat out the Santa Ana winds. I had won awards, the *Register* had run a front-page story about me, and KNBC had done a segment on me. I must have been one hell of a teacher. Back home, my eyesight having returned to normal, I grabbed the Johnnie Walker and toasted myself, two or three times as I recall.

The next morning, low on gas, I pulled into a station on Broadway and began to fill up my tank. I saw him coming out of the corner of my eye. In Laguna you develop a type of radar as to who has an address and who doesn't, and I could tell from the man's clothes he was almost certainly homeless. Keep your head down, look at the hose in your hand, maybe he will just keep walking. But if he asks for money I will give him some. I've got money, he doesn't.

He stopped. "Hello Mr. Utt, you live in Laguna now?" I looked at his face; vaguely familiar, but I could not recall the name. He sensed that and said his name and reminded me that he had been a student in my Contemporary Issues class several years before. Now I remembered him.

"Yes, my wife and I moved here in 2001."

"Would it be possible to borrow a dollar so I can get to the homeless shelter in the canyon?"

He stood in tattered work boots and dirty clothes, I stood next to my new BMW. I reached into my wallet and gave him a ten. I am not sure if he was grateful or insulted. Actually, I wondered if my ten dollars would do any good at all. Maybe he would be like that lady who wrote all those Harry Potter books, who was on welfare before she found her stride. Maybe.

One more professional I see is my therapist, to whom I will recount this story. As a teacher I often saw myself as "the sage on the stage," the great inspirer, rather than the instructor who worked one-on-one with students. I wonder if I had given him, a weak student, a little more individual attention, would he still be on his way to the homeless shelter this Thanksgiving eve?

James Utt often wonders how many more students he could have reached, but did not.

LIFE AFTER MEDICARE

THERE WAS ALWAYS a number that seemed old. When I got to that number, I would always revise it upwards, but one number seemed it could not be bumped up and that number was 65. That was the time of life where you entered your two-minute drill, trying to slow down Father Time's clock. I shot by that age three years ago. It just seemed like last month when I went to the Social Security office to file my paperwork. Remember when you were in elementary school and it seemed an eternity between Monday and Friday? Time does speed up as we get older, doesn't it?

The writer Mark Jacobson, one year younger than me, has said, "Plenty of my parts are out of warranty, or close." Having to "double pump" often to get out of my car, I feel his point. Here is a partial list of what has turned me from a young Icarus into someone who, and listen carefully you millennials, is busy gobbling up your Medicare funds: atrial fibrillation, pulmonary embolisms, torn rotator cuff, torn labrum, medial epicondylitis, and a torn meniscus. The sound of hitting a tennis ball on the sweet spot of my racquet is a distant memory.

Then there are the cosmetic changes. Less hair on your head and more in your ears and nose. We men often lose hair on our lower legs from decades of wearing tight socks, especially those mid-calf athletic socks popular in the 1980s. One of my legion of doctors told me that men's ears and noses continue to grow as they age. And most unfair of all, according to *Men's Health* magazine, a certain part of our anatomy declines in size as we age. Great. The "Golden Years."

Unfortunately, very unfortunately, I outlived my wonderful, kind and beautiful wife of 39 years.

Widowerhood at my age seems to leave two choices. One, become the secular monk that is content to look back on their life as an excellent bottle of wine, enjoyed to the last drop. Or, after a suitable and necessary period of grieving, go about the daunting experience of dating. Is "dating" the right term to use for people in their sixties? Do we "share time together?" Do we "hook up?"

After a year and a half, I decided not to go the way of the secular monk, but I did not know how to begin dating after such a long hiatus. I knew as a man, I had an unfair advantage as in our culture, it is more acceptable for a man to date a younger woman than it is for an older woman to date a younger man. But how much younger? I searched in vain for "Dating for Older Dummies."

A friend suggested an online dating service for people of a certain age. In other words, people who have been getting into Regal Theaters at reduced rates for a while now. I began the sign in process but chickened out, stopping before I uploaded a photo of myself or filled out a profile. But the service now had my email and I have been getting pictures sent to me of mature women I know nothing about. For all I know they could be Donald Trump supporters. I am urged to give them "a nudge," whatever that means.

I guess I want to meet someone the old way. Through a friend, in a class, on the tennis court if health ever returns. I could wait until my fame as a writer becomes so magnetic that women would be drawn to me. Yeah, and I could win Wimbledon next year, too.

It could be worse, though. I could have been born 100 years ago. In 1900, only 4 percent of the US population was over 65. Today it is 13 percent and in our fair town, it is 18 percent. So, as my dear mother would say, "Stop your bitching and get back to pitching." All things considered I am lucky, darn lucky to be alive and able to spend my autumn years in Laguna Beach.

Susi Q. Center is on Third Street, right?

James Utt is a retired social science teacher who has lived in Laguna Beach since 2001. He would like to win the PEN/Faulkner Award someday. He would also like to beat Roger Federer in a five-set match.

DATING CONVERSATION

HE WOULD BE hurt, probably angry, but she had to do what was right. Follow your head, not some old emotional baggage that had been weighing her down, holding her back. Conversation was approaching, a smile on his face as he neared the bench where they would start their walks around Alta Laguna Park and beyond. She would miss those facial expressions, the wink, the nod of the head, those nonverbal cues he sent out, but she would not miss the awkward silences, the pressure to come up with just the right thing to say at just the right time.

"Hey, Rachel. It's a beautiful day for a walk. The sun is out, but not too warm ... Wait why aren't you dressed in your walking clothes? You look like you're dressed for a date or something."

Rachel knew she had to get right to the point. Stumbling, hesitating would give him a chance to use his words and words gave him power.

"Con, if you only had a smart phone this could have been done so much more easily. That's the problem. I've come to see you as old, almost eccentric. This exclusively face-to-face relationship you want is just too constrictive. There are so many new ways to be with people and I need to explore those ways."

"You're leaving me after all this time, aren't you? Leaving me for

Texting. I should have been able to see this coming. I can read your eyes well, but they've been glued to your phone recently."

"Look, Con, let's not drag this out. Words hurt. We had some good times, but I have got to move on."

"To shallow Mr. Texting? Don't you see where you're headed? He'll pimp you out soon to Mr. Twitter and not long after that you'll be hooking up with Mr. Facebook. Then, just a short step to Snapchatting like a Kardashian. Swipe left, swipe right."

"That's not Snapchat, that's Tinder. You are so behind the times! And you are being mean."

"At least you can see my anger. Facing someone can be tough, but it's real. You have to face the consequences of your words."

"Text allows me to present myself as I want to be. He allows me to edit and polish before hitting 'send.' I can be a better me, the person I was meant to be."

"Rachel, when we talk, face-to-face, we listen, we look, we hear. We are empathetic, more human. People who date Texting get lost in their digital pre-performance. You are going to become afraid of being alone, of not being constantly in contact with others, no matter how shallow the subject."

"If I hook up with Text, I can be with him and be somewhere else at the same time. I can be at the Rooftop Lounge and text my friends at Nick's about how beautiful the sunset is. Remember when we saw the whales that one day? I want to share things like that."

"Yes, and we talked about the whales and what a sight it was. We laughed and held hands and shared the moment with our eyes and our words. Just us. That's all we needed."

"I was so much older then. I'm younger than that now."

"You're really going to do it then? Trade me in for the illusion of companionship? Digital connection is not friendship. You're falling for a guy who has buttons where his heart should be."

"Con, talk is messy, awkward, filled with gaps. You are just too demanding."

Just then Conversation saw Texting drive up. He stopped his car and, making no move to get out or look at Rachel, he took out his phone and began texting. Rachel's phone pinged. She looked down and smiled.

"Goodbye, Con," she said. She walked toward Texting's new car, a shiny iPhone 6s. "What an effortless new world this is. Newer is always better," she thought.

James Utt is a retired social science teacher who has been left behind in the digital dust.

REMEMBERING
NOVEMBER 1963

I WAS A junior at Tustin High School in 1963. Like most of my classmates, I was no fan of the president. I had grown up in Orange County after all. He was too soft on communism. He wanted to bring socialized medicine to the United States. We laughed at comedians who mocked his eastern accent.

It was a Friday, and our thoughts were not on the president who we believed would surely lose a bid for reelection. Plans for the weekend were being made. Many bragged about "hot" dates they had arranged. Others talked of things their family was going to do during the upcoming Thanksgiving holiday. I had not yet mustered the courage to ask a girl out on a date and my divorced mother would take us to her mother's for a small but loving Thanksgiving dinner. At least this coming Sunday, I could watch my favorite sports team, the Los Angeles Rams, on our fuzzy black-and-white television.

We were startled out of our thoughts about upcoming fun as wild rumors began to blaze across the quad. "There's some kind of prison break in Dallas." "Shots have been fired." "That's where the President is today, right?" "I heard that the Governor of Texas is dead and the President has been wounded."

By the end of lunch, the rumors had boiled down to the belief that President Kennedy had indeed been shot. No one knew how seriously though. A strange hush descended over the normally rowdy student body as we trudged up the stairs to our sixth period classes. Mrs. Brubaker was my English teacher and a rarity in Tustin: a liberal Democrat. And a great admirer of the President.

She told us in quivering tones that the teachers had received word that the President had been shot, but no one knew if he was alive or dead. There would be no teaching that day as we would await word from Dallas.

In 1963, the main building of Tustin High, a beautiful old two-story structure, would probably have crumbled into dust if a large earthquake hit. My English class looked out over the large lawn in front of the school. My desk was in the very back of the room and I often gazed out the large windows when Mrs. Brubaker failed to hold my attention.

The room that day was as quiet as if we were taking a final exam. A whisper, a note passed, nothing else, each alone with their thoughts of how the world might have just changed. Toward the end of class, I looked out the window and saw a school janitor make his way toward the flag pole in the middle of the lawn.

"Mrs. Brubaker, you should come back here," I said, breaking the silence that had held sway for thirty minutes. As I sat at my desk, she put her hand on my shoulder and strained to get a better view.

The janitor lowered the American flag to half-staff.

"Is that done if the President is only wounded?" she asked hopefully.

I knew.

"No, Mrs. Brubaker, they lower it only if the person is dead."

Warm tears spilled from her eyes onto my shirt. More tears, a muffled moan, an unsteady walk back to her desk. The rest of the class rushed to the windows and saw the flag. Now we all knew. Girls covered their faces, boys tried to affect a stoic appearance. How do 16-year-olds behave when they learn the leader of the free world has been murdered? We weren't sure.

Just before class ended, the vice principal came to our room and made a formal announcement that President John F. Kennedy had been shot dead in Dallas. Our lives, our world, had been shaken. We had questions, concerns, but no answers.

As the bell rang, we departed the distraught Mrs. Brubaker. The smartest guy in class leaned over to me and whispered, "Guess that means Goldwater has it made in the '64 election." Guess he wasn't that smart. But who is at sixteen?

Inspired by teachers like Mrs. Brubaker, James Utt became a high school teacher and taught for 38 years. He has never forgotten that day.

A CURMUDGEON LOOKS AT THANKSGIVING

I HAVE NOT let my iconoclastic, cranky side out for a walk for some time. The holiday season seems like a fine time to let loose. I wanted to write about what a stupid holiday Halloween is, but I was afraid my house would get egged. Not by angry kids, but by outraged adults who spend $1.2 billion on costumes. Americans also spend $350 million on pet costumes. Like social critic H. L. Mencken said, "No one ever went broke underestimating the taste of the American public." Not wanting to incur the wrath of candy-crazed Americans, I have decided to pick on Thanksgiving instead.

The idealized memory of that first Thanksgiving when 90 members of the Wampanoag tribe sat down to eat in friendly harmony with 50 Pilgrims is taught to every school child. This tribe, it should be remembered, gave food to the Pilgrims and taught them how to grow certain crops. Without these Native Americans, those who came over on the *Mayflower* would have experienced a difficult time surviving that first winter.

The fate that befell Native Americans after their first Thanksgiving is all too often pushed to the back of our memory. As a former social science teacher, I did my best to show students what took place.

With the arrival of the Puritans in 1630, our history took a nasty turn. Beginning with the slaughter of the Pequots and continuing to the shameful "battle" at Wounded Knee in 1890, white Americans waged a war of extermination against those they called Indians. Civil War hero General Phil Sheridan said, "The only good Indians I ever saw were dead."

If slavery is our country's original sin, our treatment of Native Americans is not far behind. We tend to forget this inconvenient truth as we sit down to our November feast.

Ah, the modern day American Thanksgiving, where, in a nation that is 37 percent obese, the average citizen consumes a meal of 4500 calories. And notice the division of labor. In most homes the women slave away in the kitchen while the menfolk watch football. Come on guys! I have taken cooking classes. I can prepare a turkey, and I always did the dishes. Are you afraid you will miss a part of the always exciting Detroit Lions game?

Some have said Thanksgiving seems to be a time when family and friends gather and remember why they don't see each other more often. The copious amounts of alcohol consumed during the day often lend themselves to nasty political fights. This year, when the two most unpopular candidates vie for the presidency, there are bound to be some real knock-down, drag-out, cover-the-kid's-ear shouting matches.

Gluttony, bad football, the drunken uncle who starts the political discussion, long travel to spend time with folks you'd rather not see—that's Thanksgiving for too many Americans. Why do we need a holiday to recognize what we are grateful for? Shouldn't that be something we are aware of every day? And, oh dear lord, what happens the next day? Black Friday and the mad rush toward an over-commercialized Christmas. But that is a subject for another column.

I know I have thrown some cold water on a beloved American holiday. There are many of you that enjoy a warm, low-key gathering where love and fellowship reign, and where husbands and sons actually help prepare and clean up. Many of you are also aware of the savagery our nation employed against its original inhabitants. To you, this curmudgeon apologizes.

But I do urge the rest of you, as you consume your turkey and pie, to not forget what happened to the Native Americans soon after that first Thanksgiving.

James Utt was last seen trying to poke holes in the Macy's Thanksgiving Day Parade balloons.

AN INFREQUENT APPEARANCE

So MANY SEASONS had come and gone since I was able to look down from my deck and see the goat herd of Laguna, but in early February, there they were. The ever-friendly herder and his loyal dog came up the slope to speak to me while he was in the process of putting up the temporary fencing that controlled where his goats could roam each day.

He explained that the goats had not been in my area for the last three years because there had not been enough rainfall to produce anything for his herd to devour. Well, last season Southern California finally got an average amount of rain, producing more edibles on Mystic Hills. Ah, the return of the herd, a wonderful sight. Not only are they reducing the risk of fire sweeping up the hillside, but are also rarely seen in our urbanized county.

I took a short trip to Las Vegas to watch Elton John perform, and upon my return the herd had finished its work and was nowhere to be seen. The hill seemed sadder for their absence, and I was sadder still when I realized it might be many seasons before I saw them again. After last season's rainfall, we in this region are back in dangerous drought-like conditions. As the *L.A. Times* recently put it, "Southern California is desperate for rain." Between February 19th of last year and February 19th of this year, Los Angeles has had one day of significant rain. One day!

Steve Johnson, long-range forecaster with Atmospherics Group International, has said if this season continues its record dryness, "California is marching into unprecedented territory, which has never been seen before in recorded climate history."

One wonders if there is a connection between California's drought and global warming?

I ran across an article in the *New York Times* that reported, "Global warming caused by human emissions has most likely intensified the drought in California by 15 to 20 percent." In the same article, Columbia professor A. Park Williams says of California's drought, "It would be a fairly bad drought no matter what. But it's definitely made worse by global warming."

By bringing up the issue of global warming, I run the risk of a partisan fight. I will take that risk because, finally, the number of Americans who believe that the planet is getting hotter as a result of human activity is growing. According to a recent Gallup poll survey, nearly 70 percent of Americans believe an increase in the Earth's temperature over the last century is mainly due to the effects of pollution.

Over 95 percent of actively publishing climate scientists agree that it is extremely likely climate warming trends over the last century are due to human activities. I could list all the scientific organizations that support this position from the American Association for the Advancement of Science to the Geological Society of America whose research has lead them to the same conclusion, but I do have a word limit for my columns.

There is the canard that all these folks are either paid to come up with this conclusion or they somehow are a minority of real scientists. Let me tell you of a scientist who was funded by the partisan Koch brothers to debunk the theory of global warming. The scientist's name is Richard Muller, and in his Koch funded study entitled,

"The Conversion of a Climate-Change Skeptic," he found that global warming was real, and humans were almost entirely the cause.

But there are still plenty of people who cling to the opposite position. One of them lives in the White House. President Trump recently said the polar ice caps are at "record levels."

Unfortunately for the president, there are groups like NASA that possess satellites who reported last year that sea ice on both poles had reached the lowest levels since data began to be recorded in 1979. Guess that news didn't make it to "Fox and Friends."

We who live in Mystic Hills should not expect to see our beloved goat herd for some time if this drought continues. This will be sad for many of us, but not a catastrophe. But it is a sign of the coming times. Think of the disappearance of the herd as a rivet on a plane that pops off. It is just one rivet, but more and more are popping off each year. How many missing rivets will it take to put the plane in real danger? Sadly, we are going to find out.

Aside from the herd and the shepherd, James Utt will miss the dog that does such a masterful job tending the flock.

A CITADEL HAS FALLEN

On November 8th, Hillary Clinton became the fifth presidential candidate to win the popular vote, yet lose the election because of the dinosaur in our Constitution known as the Electoral College.

Only time will tell if massive walls will be built, trade agreements scrapped, or "beautiful" manufacturing jobs will reappear. Who knows? Perhaps President-elect Trump will make America greater. Perhaps not. That is not the issue I address in this column.

A tectonic shift occurred in the election that might provide the disheartened Democrats of Laguna Beach and other regions of our county a ray of sunshine. Orange County voted for Hillary Clinton by a margin of 5 percent. Up until this week, no other county in California had so consistently voted Republican. It was 1936 when Democrats last came out on top, a run of 80 years. Since then, Democrats have been political road kill. In 1980 and 1984 President Reagan even won the county by fifty points. But, as Bob Dylan sang, "The times, they are a changin'."

Actually, we could sing, "The demographics, they are a changin'."

Not long ago a dear friend said to me, "What must it be like to live in an all-white Orange County, if you are not white yourself?" Now, this person is smart, but unaware of the changing face of Orange County. In 1990, whites made up two thirds of the county's population. Since I am pretty old, I can remember even further back to the 1950s and 1960s, when the percentage was even higher. I graduated from Tustin High in 1965 and our class of 700 graduates was as white as the driven snow. Visit Tustin High today and you will see quite a different student body. The sixth most populated county in the United States has changed dramatically. This has had political consequences.

With its agricultural roots and unwelcoming attitude toward unions, our county was fertile ground for strong Republicanism. An influx of conservative Midwesterners further cemented this trend. Charismatic conservative religious leaders set up shop. The county also became home to many in aerospace and defense industries. It was a potent mixture that made us one of the most reliable Republican citadels in the nation. When the orange groves began to give way to suburban homes, they were populated by families whose mothers stayed home. These women were a long way from believing Gloria Steinem's dictum, "A woman should be able to have sex before marriage and a job after."

That was then. The most recent Orange County census information is stunning. Whites make up only 44 percent of our population, while Hispanics come in at 37 percent, Asians at 17 percent, and African Africans, never a large presence here, are still only 2 percent. The last three of these demographic groups tend to vote for Democrats. Those suburban women, who used to be content with being a homemaker, are now more likely to be college educated and work outside the home. They are also less likely to be receptive to remarks that the next president said several years ago to ABC News—that putting a wife to work was a "dangerous" thing. He went on to say "… I don't want to sound too much like a chauvinist—but when I come home and dinner's not on the table, I go through the roof." Granted Mr. Trump said these things some years ago, but since his campaign dug up everything Hillary Clinton ever said, I think it only fair we apply the same standard to him.

When the British were defeated at the Battle of Yorktown, thus ensuring a colonial victory in the Revolutionary War, their band played "The World Turned Upside Down." To a small degree that is what has happened to the Orange County Republican Party.

Democrats, feel free to party like it is 1936!

James Utt is a registered independent that has voted for Republicans in some past presidential elections. He wonders where the party of George H. W. Bush went.

THE BLACK KNIGHT
HAD IT RIGHT

I RECENTLY TURNED 69. Thus begins the last year of my life when my friends can truthfully describe me to others as "A guy in his 60s." I am now flying down a freeway and the next sign has a seven and a zero on it. That is a big number, a scary number. Seventy is the new, well, seventy. A time in life when there are so many more miles behind the cart than in front of the horse.

We tend not to think of old age when we are on vacation in Kauai with our young family. Downing two or even three mai tais at dinner, up early the next morning, jogging three or four miles in the warm, sweet air of Hawaii, and then body surfing with the kids. Old age? No way, I was Dorian Gray.

But aging is a process we cannot reverse. I just did not think it would sneak up on me so quickly. It is my companion now as I am reminded each time I look in the mirror. The words of the late Andy Rooney echo in my ear, "It is paradoxical that the idea of living a long life appeals to everyone, but the idea of getting old doesn't appeal to anyone."

How then to deal with advancing age and its concomitant physical breakdowns? The devout journey to Lourdes; I go to Bushards

Pharmacy. Often. In the old TV series, *Cheers*, Norm would enter the bar, and everyone would call out his name. When I enter Bushards everyone yells out, "Jim." Blood pressure meds, blood thinners, statins, and anti-anxiety pills—just in case people post nasty comments about my column. All are provided with smiles and excellent service.

When I retired from teaching, the plan was to try my hand at writing and that has been a partial success. The other goal was to sharpen my tennis game to a fine edge. "He doesn't play like he's in his sixties." "Look at that old guy serve." "Wow, what a two-handed backhand!"

Trying to hit like you are still in your thirties comes at a price. Here is mine: partially torn rotator cuff, partially torn labrum, partially torn meniscus, and a tennis elbow operation. Throw in a reoccurring case of atrial fibrillation and my trips to the court are about as frequent as Donald Trump's trips to Black churches. If you could see me in the morning when I get out of bed, it would remind you of the Tin Man before Dorothy oiled him.

Don't go gentle into that good night. Rest, rehab, and a return to the courts! Two weeks into my comeback, I awoke with blurred vision in one eye. The ophthalmologist, who was a former student of mine, said I had a posterior vitreous detachment. It could have caused a detached retina, but did not. However, I was left with what is called a "floater" in my left eye, a gray mass that moves around as my eye moves. It is like my eye is a windshield of a car and a bug is splattered against it, except this bug moves. Bushards can't help me here.

Now, when I play tennis and it is my turn to serve, I see the ball *and* the floater. My concentration is easily broken and my serve is now a threat to low flying birds and the back of my doubles partner's head. But I will keep playing, taking as my inspiration a character from the film *Monty Python and the Holy Grail*. There is a scene where the Black Knight blocks King Arthur's path. A sword fight ensues. First, the knight loses one arm, then the other. He refuses to quit and begins to head butt the king. The fight continues and King Arthur cuts off both of his legs, reducing him to a torso. The knight looks up and says, "All right, we'll call it a draw."

In the end, it is not if we win or lose, but if we keep playing. And, yes, I will settle for a draw.

James Utt is a retired social science teacher who remembers the days of wooden racquets and short shorts on the court.

I RESOLVE, MORE OR LESS

Approximately 40 percent of Americans make New Year's resolutions. That is more than watch the Super Bowl. The University of Scranton has done research that suggests only 8 percent actually achieve their New Year's goals. Studies indicate that so many fail because they attempt extreme makeovers, such as "get fit," "lose weight," "quit smoking." For success in sticking to your resolutions, I recommend keeping them simple.

One expert says the best resolution you can make is to get more sleep. It not only makes you feel better, but also enhances the chance of achieving your other resolutions. Sorry, but at age 69, I tend to roll with Ben Franklin who slept only four hours a night and believed there was enough time for sleeping in the grave.

So, not wanting to make grand resolutions I probably cannot live up to, I resolve to do the following smaller things:

I resolve to eat one vegetarian meal a week. Oh, come on man, who are you kidding? I resolve to eat one vegetarian meal a month. Wait. That still sounds like I would be subjecting myself to enhanced interrogation techniques. Okay, I resolve to eat one vegetarian meal a year. If I put bacon bits on a salad, can it still be counted as vegetarian?

I resolve to hit my tennis forehand with more topspin so it will not hit the net as often. By the way, if I am ever found murdered, tell the police my doubles partner had motive.

I resolve to be less snarky in my columns about Newport Beach and its residents. If you are a betting person, you should bet that I break this resolution first. Some targets are so, so inviting.

I resolve not to think poorly of tourists who come to our town. Everyone has an inalienable right to wear black knee socks with sandals.

I resolve to not take living in Laguna Beach, with all its beauty and charm, for granted. When my wife and I moved here in 2001, we were struck every morning and evening by the gorgeous view. We saw the village below, San Clemente Island on a clear winter's day, purple clouds at sundown. All too often, I walk past my windows without an appreciative glance. No more. I was recently at a dinner party and met a couple that lives on Lido Island on the bay side. I thought, "Ah, those poor souls." *There goes the resolution about Newport Beach.*

I resolve to attend LagunaTunes concerts because they bring a spirit of joy and happiness to our town twice a year.

I resolve to buy books only at Laguna Beach Books, one of our city's true treasures.

I resolve to attend school board meetings, even though I have no children in the school system.

This would merely be an act of good citizenship. The board is in the hands of dedicated and competent people and I would like to make myself more aware of their good efforts.

I resolve not to avoid the eyes of the homeless who share our town as I pass them on the streets. If I were a Christian, I would say we are brothers and sisters in Christ. Since I am not, I will simply look upon them as my fellow human beings who, by illness or bad fortune, have fallen on hard times. If they ask for help, I will give it.

Lastly, I resolve, if President Trump appoints judges to the Supreme Court who will overturn Roe v. Wade and marriage equality, break up families with deportation forces, and ignore the danger of climate change, I will devote what energies I have to help make him a one-term president.

If all else fails, just remember you live in Laguna Beach, rated as the city with the lowest obesity rate in America. Happy New Year!

James Utt resolved to quit smoking in 1977 and has not had a cigarette since. He misses them every day.

JANUS, JANUARY AND AN AMERICAN HERO

It is January, named for the Roman god Janus, he of two faces. One face was so he could look backwards, the other forwards. If old Janus is still looking backward these days, he would have to shield his eyes from much of what happened in the past year.

The continuing hell of Aleppo, Czar Vladimir the First gaining power around the world as he snuffs out freedom at home, and the guy with the world's worst haircut and clothes, playing with nukes in North Korea. In our own country, we had to deal with Zika, the Dallas police shooting, and the slaughter in Orlando. Many of us in Laguna hold our breath as we see how our next president, who seems to favor communication in 140 characters or less, handles the world's toughest job.

But it is a new year, so let us look through Janus's forward face. What historical events took place in this month that we can take note of, be proud as Americans that they happened? Albeit, many of them later than they should have.

January 23, 1849 was the day that the first woman was awarded a medical degree in the United States. Elizabeth Blackwell was so certified by the Medical Institute of Geneva, New York. Today nearly half of American medical students are female.

Nellie Tayloe Ross became the first female governor when she was sworn in on January 5, 1925. She governed the beautiful state of Wyoming. Since then forty women have served as governors.

It was not until 1966 that our country had an African American cabinet member, when on January 18th of that year, LBJ tapped Robert Clifton Weaver to be HUD secretary. Ironically, President Trump has selected another African American, Dr. Ben Carson, to hold this same post. Strange, it was just in November when Dr. Carson said he was too inexperienced to run a federal agency.

It took until January 13, 1990 that our country had its first African American governor. This honor went to Douglas Wilder as the people of Virginia made him their chief executive. You might ask how many African American governors we have had since then. Wait while I count them up. One.

I love college football, so I am aware that Clemson University in South Carolina is a national power. It reminds me that on January 28, 1963, Harvey Gantt became the first African American to be admitted to that university. South Carolina was one of the last states to integrate its universities. This is not too hard to understand when you remember this is the state that gave us senators and governors like John C. Calhoun, the murderous "Pitchfork" Ben Tillman, and Strom Thurmond, he of the "Dixiecrat" Party. Gantt went on to be the first black mayor of Charleston and later to run unsuccessfully for senator against Jesse Helms, who led a filibuster in the US Senate against making Martin Luther King's birthday a national holiday.

Finally, there is January 15, 1929, the day Martin Luther King was born. Although it is not always celebrated on that day. We move it around so we can have that most American of events, the three-day weekend.

I dare you, Janus dares you, to find me an American outside of the Klan who is still not electrified by King's "I Have a Dream" speech.

Inspiring and hopeful, it was a call to action. Like Gandhi before him he led the fight against injustice. Like Gandhi, he paid for this with his life. Let us remember him this January and hope another such as him will rise to inspire us to overcome our divisions. Let me leave you with one of my favorite sayings from this great American: "Darkness cannot drive out darkness; only light can do that. Hate cannot drive out hate; only love can do that."

Look forward.

James Utt is a retired teacher who has lived in Laguna since 2001. He misses the idealism of the 1960s.

WHAT YOU CAN DO
FOR YOUR COUNTRY

THANKSGIVING, AS WELL as Newport Beach, has felt the slings and arrows of this columnist. The new president; Dana Rohrabacher; and those that kill whales have come under scrutiny and ridicule as well. Now, new targets of opportunity need to be found. A couple present themselves. With advancing age comes wisdom and insight, or maybe just crankiness, but I would like to do the dance of ideas with Laguna High School seniors and libertarians.

High school seniors wait this time of year with bated breath to see if they have been accepted at the college of their choice. The angst, the sleepless nights. An end can be put to this suffering. Instead of sweating out the word from an admissions office, seniors should be thinking about which type of national service they will enter for the next one to two years. That's right. I propose the United States enact a compulsory national service law for all graduating seniors or those who have dropped out and are now 18.

Citizenship is a balance between rights and responsibilities, and the pendulum in contemporary America has swung far too much in the direction of the former. Everyone demands their rights, but what do we owe in return for the vast array of freedoms we enjoy?

Take the military as an example. In 1975, 70 percent of members of Congress were veterans. Today, less than 20 percent are, and only a tiny fraction of their children are in uniform. Less than half of one percent of Americans is in active military service. This minuscule group goes on tour after tour in dangerous lands while the rest of us stay safely at home. If a larger and broader cross section of Americans served in our armed forces, we might be more judicious when engaging in foreign adventures.

My national service bill would not require everyone to serve in the military. If you don't want to be in uniform, no problem. There would be a number of options, all of which would fulfill your requirement. The Peace Corps and AmeriCorps VISTA come to mind. Existing charitable organizations could expand their base of operations. One might build homes for Habitat for Humanity, help maintain our national parks, or work in assisted living facilities. By the way, you would be paid for this work, just as those in the military would.

I can hear the libertarians' cries of "involuntary servitude," and "the government cannot force us to do these things." Please. We compel our citizens to pay taxes, educate their kids, and report for jury duty. For the well being of others and our country, more needs to be asked from the people lucky enough to be Americans. Right now, we are a very divided nation. Graduates need to discover that we do have things in common with people outside of the privileged bubble of Laguna Beach. It would enrich our lives and make our nation stronger if we served together, worked together, and learned from each other.

Not long ago, General Stanley McChrystal said, "… I believe every young person deserves … the experience of being part of something larger than themselves." National service would provide this opportunity.

Dear Laguna Beach High School seniors, I know many of you could make a seamless transition to a top-level university and flourish. But having taught seniors for 35 years, I know all too well that many of you are not ready. Whether you are prepared or not to take what you see as your next step, I urge you to think about the good you could do for our nation and yourselves by devoting a year or two to serving our country. Please keep in mind the words that President Kennedy said that cold morning in 1961, "Ask not what your country can do for you, but what you can do for your country."

Young people, you have a long life ahead of you. Don't make the mistake of believing your life belongs exclusively to you.

James Utt served in the United States Army from 1971 to 1974. He is a better citizen because of that experience.

LAGUNA IN BLACK-AND-WHITE

AT MY AGE, the mind and body must make an extra effort to stay active. Having realized that a defeat of Roger Federer in a grueling five-set match is most likely never going to happen, a new avocation has taken hold of me. Photography.

I have not used a camera since my time in the service in the 1970s, when old Korean men were reluctant to have their pictures taken for fear part of their soul might be captured on the film. But walking through town, one sees too many scenes that deserve to be captured and preserved. I feel a burning desire to start taking pictures again. So I procured a used camera—film, of course. No digital for this Luddite, besides the people at the photo shop said film is making a comeback and for the type of photography I want to do, film would be just fine.

Oh, and in another nod to the old school, I want to shoot in black-and-white. I will never be another Ansel Adams, or Avedon, but to me their work has a beauty and complexity that transcends the colors of nature. Researching why one should shoot in black-and-white, I ran across phrases like "color can be distracting," "you get a stronger emotional connection to the subject," "there is more feeling." These may be true, but I just know that black-and-white pictures speak to me with more power and a greater sense of reality. There is also a beauty that color does not capture. Colorless it will be.

So what scenes of opportunity present themselves in Laguna Beach for my used Canon and me?

The homeless come first to mind. Some might say it is an intrusion into what privacy they have left. But their presence needs to be catalogued, so they will not become invisible to those of us who live here. Returning to Laguna late after our most recent "Hospitality Night," the winds whipping, the streets now empty of revelers, I saw them in the shadows, moving as if they would rather not be seen. Their few possessions were on their backs or held tightly in their arms. I was reminded of a poem by Wilfred Owen about exhausted soldiers in World War I returning to their lines after a mission. "Bent double, like old beggars under sacks." They are here, whether in the shadows, hiding from the light, or on the benches in front of the library. Black-and-white would show them with power and a shred of dignity that they are all too often denied.

Early morning in our town offers fertile ground for shooting in black-and-white. My home is in Mystic Hills, looking across the way at Temple Hills. Many mornings, the white fog makes its way up Park Avenue, its tendrils snaking toward Thurston Middle School. The contrast with the darker hills that the fog envelops is breathtaking.

Another shot could be of that first surfer braving the winter's cold to paddle out at Thalia, or Forest Avenue just waking up before the tidal wave of humanity engulfs its sidewalks. Perhaps a toddler holding his mother's hand as he puts his toes in the ocean for the very first time might make a memorable picture.

Black-and-white would capture the sadness of the now closed Cafe Zoolu where so many of us ate the best swordfish on the planet. Speaking of restaurants, I wish the Cottage was still there to shoot. Bad coffee, great memories.

If I can ever stay up that late, a shot of the Marine Room Tavern at "last call" might be an interesting one.

And people, always people. Whether it is locals who love this town or tourists with sun burned faces, walking back to their cars with kids in tow knowing they will return. Black-and-white does capture a piece of their soul and their beauty.

James Utt hopes that if a gray-haired man with an old Canon asks to take your picture you will not be offended.

SHINING CITY

ONE OF THE advantages of being in the autumn of my years is that I can look back over several decades and report firsthand on dramatic changes that have affected our nation. One might think that technological change would be the first thing that comes to mind. But this is not a column about Kindles or iPads, or "I remember when a person actually had to get up from the sofa to change the television station." Changes of the heart and mind are of more consequence.

Growing into young manhood in the United States in the 1950s and 1960s, I, like almost everyone else, was taught that "queers" were to be avoided, feared, and ridiculed. These *homosexuals* seemed to be of two types, at least in the male gender. One was the effeminate pansy that would shriek at the sudden appearance of a spider. The other was the leather-clad brute that would do unspeakable things to Bible-believing boys from Tustin.

We were told to stay clear of Laguna Beach because it was "queer central." Even their high school sports teams were called the "Artists," and we all knew that most artistically inclined people were most likely "homos." Our Tustin football players would hurl manly insults across the line of scrimmage at the Laguna players. We did not stop to think that our own mascot, the "Tiller," would not strike fear into anyone or anything except perhaps an unplowed field.

That was then. But how things have changed. Perhaps the Stonewall Riots of 1969 ignited a small spark. Maybe the more tolerant sexual attitudes of the 1970s and 1980s caused the spark to grow into a flame. Undoubtedly the agony of the AIDS epidemic that ravaged the gay community caused a softening of America's heart. But when *Will and Grace* became an established television hit in 1998, we knew America was not living in our fathers' world any longer. I suspect it came down to the fact that more Americans realized that they knew people who were gay, or that their best friend's son or daughter was gay. In the interests of full disclosure, I should mention I have two sons, one of whom is gay. I have, therefore, seen the effects of homophobia, which is still strong in certain quarters, up close and personal.

Through all these difficult times, there was our Laguna Beach, a haven for those who would have been scorned in practically any other community. Our city nurtured a strong, proud gay community that was, yes, artistic, as well as tolerant and welcoming. Laguna Beach had the first openly gay mayor in the nation, and now, we are on the verge of taking another important step.

The May 12th issue of the *Indy* had a front-page article that informed readers that the City Council had voted to make June the annual Lesbian, Gay, Bisexual and Transgender Heritage and Culture Month. The moving force behind this was the Laguna Beach LGBT Heritage & Culture Committee, which was established by realtor Chris Tebbutt. Once again, in the interests of full disclosure, I should mention that Chris was a student of mine at El Toro High School. However, I can lay no claim to having shaped his decency or diligence.

The committee wants to preserve stories of Laguna's gay history and recognize the many contributions that the Laguna LGBTQ community has made to our city.

John Winthrop, the first governor of the Massachusetts Bay Colony, spoke of creating "a shining city on a hill" that would be an example for all others. It is sadly ironic that he hated democracy and was religiously intolerant, but that is a story for another day. In a way we can look at our Laguna Beach as a shining city on a hill, because it stood for so long, unrecognized by so many, as a true place of tolerance and welcoming. Let us remember with pride the history of our city.

Chris, thank you for the work you and others are doing.

James Utt would like to remind you that our congressman is against marriage equality.

FRIENDS DON'T LET FRIENDS

SOMETIMES PEOPLE INSULT you, but they are not intentionally trying to be mean. They are just doing their job with no ill intent. They think they are being efficient, thorough, or polite. But the unintended insult still stings.

I never ask for a senior discount at the movies. Not wanting to announce to those in line behind me that I am, well, old, I pay extra for pride's sake. One afternoon, dressed in my newest Tommy Bahamas and with just the right amount of hair product, I waited in line to see a matinee. When it was my turn at the window, I handed the young lady a twenty. She gave me a ticket and said, "Here is your change for one senior ticket." I was betrayed by my own wrinkled face and thinning gray hair. The employee saw, with her young eyes, that I was eligible for the near-death discount. Only extra butter on my popcorn could soothe the pain. I sat in the back row so none could see the creeping bald spot on the back of my head that must have been expanding by the minute.

That hurt, but not as much as what happened shortly after. Man needs steak to live and I had just ordered one, rib eye, of course, at a fairly good restaurant in town. Thinking a hearty red would be the best complement to this meal, I ordered a Zinfandel. The server looked at me with a kindly smile and asked, "Will that be white Zinfandel, sir?"

The world suddenly stopped spinning on its axis. The week before the ticket taker had outed me as an old person. Now this? Did I look like a person who drank white Zinfandel? I had brought a copy of the *New York Review of Books* to read. This alone should have exempted me from such a question. I don't actually read it much, but it impresses the hell out of people at nearby tables. Was the server unable to see that I was not a young person who wanted something sweet for a cheap buzz?

"Do I look like the type of person who would drink white Zinfandel? You have put an arrow through my heart," I said, with a smile. She wasn't wearing a wedding ring and perhaps a connection could be made here, despite her hurtful question.

"Well, I have to be sure, because a lot of tourists are in town for the festivals and a number of women like to drink it." She was to show no further interest in what she probably perceived as a wine snob. A wine snob who was trying to chat up a much younger woman.

But, white Zinfandel? As Chris Carter used to say on ESPN when there was a real blooper on the field, "Come on, man!"

White Zinfandel is a cheap wine made with low quality sugary grapes. Wine, and liquor in general, are not made to be sweet. Some, more generous than I, cut white Zin drinkers some slack by saying it is a gateway wine that will put them, in time, on a pathway to better wines. But I see these drinkers caught in a web from which they will never escape. They will forever crave the sweet, fruity taste. They will have as comrades all those underage drinkers who want to get drunk, but do not want to taste the liquor. I can't say for sure, but I would not be surprised if the stars of *Duck Dynasty* wash down their kills with goblets of white Zin.

Oh, the humanity. Rosé, made from the blend of early red grapes, nearly destroyed Western Civilization. Now, white Zin is emerging as a new threat. Think of all the poor yeasts that will give their last full measure of devotion to the creation of this type of wine. The New Testament says Jesus' first miracle was turning water into wine. I would be really disappointed if that wine was white Zin.

All wines are not created equal. And one that is not equal is white Zin. If you ever get a bottle as a gift, know that the gift giver knows nothing about wine. Or they simply hate you.

There have to be standards or society crumbles. Say it with me, brothers and sisters of the vine,

"Friends do not let friends drink white Zinfandel!"

As you might guess, one of James Utt's favorite books is William Henry's In Defense of Elitism.

THE BIGFOOT BAR

EVERY YEAR, FRIENDS and family suggest that I get out of town during the summer months to avoid the choking traffic and tourist onslaught that engulfs us. I tell them, with apologies to John Milton, "Better to suffer in Laguna than relax anywhere else."

But this year, I decided to get away for a few days and visit one of my sons who left the bright lights of Burbank for life in rural Washington, specifically Roy, Washington, population 800. Monday through Friday, he cuts down trees. On the weekends, he gives guitar lessons. Chainsaws to guitar picks, the Renaissance Man of Roy.

He and his wife picked me up at the Seattle airport. Our journey to their home went from freeway, to four-lane highway, to two-lane highway, to, finally, a small paved road with no white line down the middle. I have never seen so many trees. The forests were so dense that Bigfoot and his entire family could have been ten feet off the road and I would have never seen them.

Money goes a long way in rural America. Their two-story house sits on an acre of land, with its own well, a cherry tree, an apple tree, and other trees this city boy cannot name. Mount Rainier, still covered in snow, is visible from their property. Roaming the grounds are a magnificent Newfoundland-Lab mix, two pooped out pugs, and one vicious cat that managed to kill a bird and a rabbit during my stay. He did this not because he was hungry but because, like most cats, he is a serial killer.

One day during my stay, my son took me to a classic car show in the small town of Eatonville, which is close to Mount Rainier. His wife did mention that Mount Rainier is still an active volcano and, if it blows, Eatonville would be destroyed. But Rainier remained quiet and I got to see some great old cars and visit with their friendly owners. They told me about their cars' special parts, and ways they had customized them. I nodded my head knowingly, but understood practically nothing they were talking about. A car guy, I am not.

No visit to Eatonville would be complete without a visit to the Bigfoot Bar. So, after viewing the cars, in we went. I instantly realized I should not have packed like someone who lives in a Southern California beach town. There I stood in a Tommy Bahama shirt and shorts with Sperry topsiders on my feet. I was surrounded by loggers, motor heads, and people who actually shoot animals for food. They were dressed, ah, differently. They had calluses on their hands and no one was drinking a Corona with a lime stuck in it. I must admit, I felt a warmer vibe there than in the bar at Javier's in Crystal Cove.

My son's neighbors have horses, pigs, sheep, and goats. This Laguna resident was in the country now, but not so far into the country as to be out of Walmart range. Confession: I had never been in a Walmart before. I can now cross that one off my bucket list. In size it rivaled St. Peter's Basilica. We were there to buy a small wading pool for a cookout to be given in my honor, the night before my departure from Roy. There would be some small children in attendance, thus the need for the pool.

Alright, key rule at a party where you don't know most of the people: Do not talk politics or religion. This is especially true in "Make America Great Again" territory. I obeyed this dictum and even refrained from correcting double negatives that seemed to increase as the beer flowed. I did, however, step in it, so to speak, in two other unrelated areas. I made a wise guy crack about country music; something to the effect that "country music" was a contradiction in terms.

And, more dangerously, I degraded the Seattle Seahawks. This is blasphemy in Washington and I had to beat a hasty retreat.

To visit my son and his wife was joyous. To see new places and meet people who have been shaped by different experiences is something of great value, especially for someone born and raised behind the Orange Curtain. There will be a return to Roy in the future, this time with clothes more befitting the area. But, as I sat in the Seattle airport waiting for my flight home, I must confess I was not humming "Take Me Home, Country Roads," but rather "Take Me to Laguna Beach, Alaska Airlines."

During the cookout, someone pushed the murderous cat into the wading pool. James Utt swears he did not do it.

EARLY MORNING RISER

"EARLY MORNING RISER" was a song recorded in 1972 by the group Pure Prairie League. Sweet and soulful, with Craig Fuller singing lead, "Riser" is as fine a country rock tune as you will hear.

Recently, on weekends, I have become an early morning riser. This is partly due to my obnoxious cat that makes death rattle meows as soon as the sky begins to shed the slightest shade of darkness. However, my main reason for rolling out of bed so early is my recent interest in photography.

I want to catch Laguna Beach before it becomes midtown Manhattan.

In July and August, I am downtown by 5:30, camera in hand. To quote another classic rock song, this one by the Rolling Stones, "It was so very quiet and peaceful, there was nobody, not a soul around." Well, that is not entirely accurate, but pretty close. I can stand in the crosswalk in front of the Hotel Laguna and not see a single car on PCH. It is a "peaceful easy feeling," but I know in two hours this stretch of pavement will resemble the Indianapolis 500.

I come upon another empty street. This time standing in front of the fire station, looking down Forest. There are no cars, moving or parked. Only the no-armed bandits, I mean the city's parking meters, waiting like Venus flytraps to ensnare unsuspecting tourists.

There are other early morning risers. Across from Tommy Bahama there is a frail homeless man with a pathetically weathered broom and a long-handled dustpan. Oblivious to my presence, this unofficial sanitary engineer sweeps the space where the street meets the curb. I believe he is doing this as a service to the city that allows him some degree of residence.

Walking north on PCH, I come to the gas station on Broadway, the one with the mini mart. No one is at the pumps yet. My mind flashes back to this place a few years ago. Filling up my shiny new German car, I was approached by a man who asked for a dollar to help get him to the shelter in the canyon. As I fumbled for my wallet he said, "So Mr. Utt, do you live in Laguna now?" He was a former student.

Half past six is probably too early for the spinning sidewalk surfer of Brooks Street, but I drive over anyway. Perhaps he is doing a sunrise service this Saturday. He is not, but across the street, slowly walking north, is another homeless person. Wrapped so tightly in tattered clothes it is difficult to tell the sex of this early morning riser. Using my zoom lens, I see I am looking at a woman. She is passing a window that says, "Weddings Parties Events." Jarring juxtaposition, as she is very unlikely to attend any such gatherings.

There are people up and about, other than the homeless this day. There are the joggers, dog walkers, and the guy with the metal detector, searching for whatever treasures the sand might yield.

There are also divers getting scuba gear ready. Most seem to have six pack abs and bulging biceps.

I have to suppress a strong desire to hate them. The envy of the old for the young is a powerful force.

In the end, the natural beauty of Laguna Beach in the early morning hours is what takes my breath away. People are precious, but the photos I take without them move me in a deeper way. Crescent Bay at sunrise, the lonely emptiness of the Laguna Cinema with its missing letters, the waves striking the rocks at Cress Street at low tide, a bird standing watch on the post of a volleyball court. Especially beautiful are agave americana plants, often called century plants, growing tall and bold against the early morning sun. These are the things that draw me from my bed so early with my used Canon and rolls of black-and-white film.

Our town is among the best places to live in the world. But, all too often, we are inundated with people. Think about setting your alarm for just before sunrise some Saturday or Sunday, stumble out of bed, no shower necessary, and see Laguna before rush hour. It is worth the missed sleep.

Don't tell the police, but James Utt jaywalks across PCH early in the morning.

WAS IT MY TURN?

THOSE OF YOU that have been kind enough to read my columns the past couple of years may have noticed that each October, which is Breast Cancer Awareness Month, I write about the disease that killed my wife. This year, there is a more personal touch to my writing.

My cardiologist did not like certain aspects of my blood work, so he said I should see a "blood doctor." "Hematologist" could now be added to the legion of healers visited in the past twenty years. Dialing the number of the doctor he recommended, the only words I remember the receptionist saying were "Cancer Center." The doctor I was being referred to was not a hematologist, but an oncologist. The cardiologist must have suspected something more was afoot.

Oncologists tend to work in groups and thus have large office space and huge waiting rooms. All the time spent with my wife in such places is a reoccurring nightmare. Chairs filled with people in the fight of their lives, a fight many, if not most, would lose. Sitting in my seat in this unhappy place, waiting for my name to be called, I wondered if it was my turn to enter the ring with a disease that does not lose many fights, but earns a victory after countless rounds of chemo.

"Why didn't I eat more fish, why didn't I drink less, why didn't I eat more leafy greens, why ...?"

"Mr. Utt," the nurse called.

The oncologist was a jolly old elf who immediately put me at ease. He asked many questions, reviewed my medical records from other doctors, and gave me a brief physical exam. He patted my knee and said, "I am going to order lots of tests for you, not because I found anything, but just to be sure."

That was reassuring, but can you trust jolly elves? Was he trying to keep a very nervous man from more sleepless nights? I remember all the calming things said to my wife during her last years.

During the next week, I had enough blood drawn for use in a good slasher movie. I had scans. I waited in the cold reception room once again.

"Mr. Utt."

The doctor entered the exam room with papers showing the results of my tests. "We will check it again in three months. Then maybe, maybe, a type of infusion and a bone scan. But no big problem we need to act on right now," he said reassuringly.

I felt my blood pressure lower, and thought briefly about kissing him on the lips. The euphoria lasted until my exit through the waiting room where sat people who I was sure would not receive the relatively good news just given to me.

Cancer kills about 1500 Americans every twenty-four hours. That is like a *Titanic* going down every day, a 9/11 every two days. By year's end, over half a million deaths due to cancer will have occurred.

When asked what will cure cancer, one oncologist answered, "Money." More fortunate than most, I am able to give significant sums to the Breast Cancer Research Foundation to aid their tireless work in finding a cure. But, I am not most people. Here is where our government needs to play a leading role. The Preamble to the Constitution speaks of, among other things, "promoting the general welfare."

Certainly, fighting the scourge of cancer would fall under promoting the general welfare.

That is why I was so discouraged to see President Trump's proposed budget call for a one-billion-dollar reduction for the National Cancer Institute. That is a 19 percent reduction. Dr. Daniel Hayes, past president of the American Society of Clinical Oncology, said recently, "Such extreme reductions to programs that are critical to research will fundamentally damage our nation's progress in treating patients."

The President's budget, as he promised, included a healthy increase for defense, even though we currently spend more than the next seven countries combined. But the budget blueprint calls for a $5.8-billion cut to the National Institutes of Health. Seems like we *may* be safer, but also sicker, if this budget is adopted.

Perhaps Mick Mulvaney, head of the Office of Management and Budget, and President Trump could think just a little more about all those people in the cancer center waiting rooms.

James Utt hopes he is not one of the 1.6 million Americans diagnosed with cancer this year.

A WHALE OF A COMEBACK

How DO I love thee Laguna Beach? Let me count the ways. Actually, there are too many to name, so let me mention just one. We are fortunate enough to live in a region where whale watching is as easy as keeping a sharp eye peeled seaward at certain times of the year.

Whales are nature in its grandest form. They are massive, beautiful, and powerful. They are gentle, inquisitive, and sentient, with a high level of intelligence. And, like humans, they are mammals that breathe air, are warm-blooded, and nurse their babies with milk. Scientists say they grieve when one of their own dies. Unfortunately, due to man's literal interpretation of Genesis where God gives humans "dominion" over all creatures, whales have had to grieve a great deal over the centuries.

Take the mighty sperm whale as an example. Between the 18th and 20th centuries, approximately one million of these magnificent creatures were slaughtered. Melville did well in making the vengeful Moby Dick this type of whale. Ahab had it coming.

Let us turn to a happier story. The type of whale we are most likely to see off our shores is the gray whale. This great creature engages in the longest migration of any mammal on earth, up to 10,000 miles, from Alaska to the warm waters off Baja California.

There, they mate and give birth. During their migration, they often come close to shore, providing a breathtaking sight.

Grays used to be found in three areas across the globe. One group, the North Atlantic gray group, is gone. That leaves the western Pacific grays and our own eastern Pacific grays. The western grays were hunted to near extinction by the 1970s, their numbers estimated to be in the low hundreds at best. Our eastern grays seemed headed for the same fate, being hunted to near extinction, when in 1986, the International Whaling Commission banned commercial whaling. However, the IWC is a voluntary organization not backed up by treaty. Fortunately, Canada, the United States, and Mexico have pledged to refrain from commercial whaling. This has been great news for eastern grays as their herds have grown to the point that, in 1995, they were removed from the endangered species list. Now over 20,000 make the long trip from Alaska to their breeding grounds in Baja. I have been close to grays while on my brother-in-law's boat. Recently we came across a mother and calf swimming gently northward; an awe-inspiring sight as the mother spouted, followed by the smaller spout of the calf. All I could think of was, "be safe, be happy, and live long."

Generations to come will be able to enjoy viewing the gray whale migration, a proud achievement for all Americans. Other types of whales are not so lucky. Some nations ignore the ban or say they are whaling for "scientific purposes." Let the record show that Japan, Norway, and Iceland are the top three nations that slay the most whales annually. Our planet is poorer for it.

Let me end by relating a personal story. My wife died in 2013. In accordance with her wishes, I deposited the urn with her ashes off the coast of Emerald Bay where she grew up. Just as I was lowering the urn overboard a blue whale breached not far from our boat. Blues are the largest creature ever to inhabit the earth and can live up to 100 years. In the pre-whaling days, they numbered over 200,000, but like so many of their kind, have suffered unjustly at the hands of man. Today, just 20,000 remain. Seeing this great creature as I was saying a final good bye to my wife gave me pause. Like the character Tyrion Lannister in *Game of Thrones*, I have been a cynic most of my life. I doubt most notions, from the afterlife to the goodness of humanity. But, I want to believe that the appearance of the great whale, at the moment I lowered my wife into her watery resting place, was not a coincidence.

James Utt agrees with Jane Velez Mitchell, who wrote, "Nature did not put whales on this earth to splash kids while stuck in a pen."

THE IDIOT AND THE DEA

"MR. UTT, THIS is Agent Fuentes of the Drug Enforcement Agency. Your name has come up in a drug investigation. Could you please call me back at your earliest convenience?" When I heard this message, my first thought was that they needed my help in nailing some low-life drug dealer. Then, I realized that I did not know any low-life drug dealers. Curiosity followed by concern began to gnaw at me. I dialed the number.

"Yes, Mr. Utt, thank you for calling back. I will get right to the point. We know that you have been purchasing drugs online from foreign pharmacies without proper prescriptions."

Oh, oh, he had me there. Because of the heart medications my cardiologist prescribed, it was becoming harder to, well, get hard. Until I got up enough courage to ask him for a prescription for Viagra, online pharmacies were very convenient. Since I was also dealing with a wife who had cancer, Prozac seemed like something that might take the edge off, and I ordered that as well. Once, when one of my relatives was having a hard time with nerves because of a new high-stress job, I purchased some Xanax for him. The authorities at the San Francisco airport intercepted this shipment and they sent me a letter saying, and, here I am paraphrasing, "Don't try this shit again, or you'll be in fucking big trouble." Since that time, I have not ordered any drugs online.

Agent Fuentes read me a list of everything I had illegally received by using these foreign outlets. He even had, what seemed to me, the correct dates. How did the DEA get this information? Did they hack into the databases of the pharmacies? But, I never did get the Xanax, and why the fuss over some boner pills for an aging baby boomer? Then, the hammer came down.

"Mr. Utt, your orders have been filled by various groups in the Dominican Republic. These groups are involved in smuggling cocaine and heroin into the United States and we believe you have been assisting them. You placed a phony order for Viagra or Prozac, yet these other drugs were brought into the US under your name."

"Look, Agent Fuentes, I have never received anything but these ED drugs or Prozac. I have never been involved in any way in smuggling hard drugs into this country."

"Unfortunately, the evidence we have points the other way. You live on Tahiti Ave., correct?"

"Yes." They knew everything about me: phone number, address, drugs used. I felt on the spot. If I was on one of those cop shows, I would crack like an egg in the interrogation room.

"There is a Suburban within a mile of your house with four agents. They have a warrant for your arrest, as well as a search warrant."

Fear, unlike any I had ever known, washed over my body. But, the worst was yet to come.

"Mr. Utt, because this crime originated in the Dominican Republic, they have jurisdiction in this affair. After your arrest, you will be extradited to that country tomorrow and face a ten-year prison term. They take these crimes very seriously as they wrestle to control the drug trade."

"This, this can't be right. All I did was order some fairly safe drugs for my own use. I was never, ever, part of a cocaine smuggling plot."

"The officials in the Dominican Republic believe they have enough evidence to lock you away. We in the DEA do our best to cooperate with them in their struggle. Do you currently have any drugs in your house?"

Oh, shit. I had some old Prozac in my sock drawer. I grabbed the bottle and flushed them down the toilet.

"Mr. Utt, it sounds like you are disposing of drugs right now."

"No, Agent Fuentes, I am so nervous I had to go to the bathroom. That is the flush you heard."

"Mr. Utt, do you have any firearms in your home? I want my agents to be safe when they arrive."

"No, absolutely no guns. Listen, Agent Fuentes, my wife has cancer, a very serious case of cancer. I cannot be taken away from her and flown down to the Dominican Republic. She needs me. Please."

"You should have thought of that before you helped drug smugglers bring these dangerous substances into our country. You have no one to blame but yourself."

My heart was pounding. I saw myself, my raggedy old ass, being raped over and over again by men in some horrible Dominican prison. I would die there. Cancer and stress would kill my wife. Would I ever see my sons again? Would they believe I was part of a drug smuggling ring?

I begged and pleaded for another five minutes. I pointed out that I had not ordered anything online in years. Was it my imagination or was he softening just a little? Was he feeling sorry for the guy whose wife had cancer? Was I convincing him that I was innocent?

Finally, he said, "I need to speak to the district attorney."

When he came back on the line, he said, "I have some good news. Since you have not ordered any drugs in the last three years, the district attorney is offering you a deal. He is willing to let you off with a fine of $3500."

"Yes, yes, I will pay that. Where do I deliver the check?"

"No, Mr. Utt, I will give you instructions on where to wire the money."

Then it hit me that I was a big, fucking idiot.

"Agent Fuentes, what is the name of the district attorney?"

"I am afraid I am not at liberty to give you his name. You must decide quickly to accept this deal or my agents will soon be at your house. Your wife may not even know where you have gone."

I was now 90 percent sure this was a scam and "Agent Fuentes" was no more a DEA guy than I was a brain surgeon.

He sensed my hesitation. "If you try and flee, my agents will catch you and the deal is off."

I hung up the phone and ran to my car. Only it was not my lightning-fast BMW, but some puny-ass loaner. Nevertheless, still thinking there was a 10 percent chance that the agents were near, I floored that little piece of shit and flew down Park Avenue. When I went down the Third Street hill, I was going so fast my head banged on the roof of the car. I ran into the sheriff's office and breathlessly told the desk sergeant that I was pretty sure I was being played by a man impersonating a federal agent.

She said, "Think about it, Mr. Utt. This is the USA. You cannot be extradited overnight without due process. They don't let you off by wiring money to some strange account. This is indeed a scam." I gave her the number of Agent Fuentes, but no one picked up when she dialed. "He has caller I.D. and knows that the Laguna police are calling. No way they will pick up. Go home and relax. But, if any strange people come around, call us at this number."

I drove past my house a couple of times to make sure there was not a Suburban lurking nearby. I phoned my son and told him what had happened. He asked for the number that the "agent" called from. When he punched it into his computer, a website popped up where people had posted about this scam. Some had actually paid the money and now felt foolish. The scam was so widespread that the real DEA had left a number. People were encouraged to call and report extortion attempts. I called and sheepishly admitted to an agent what had taken place. He was understanding, and admitted that the DEA was having trouble halting this scam, because it was well organized and centered in the Dominican Republic. They even used names of real agents. I promised that I would never buy drugs online again. He said that was a very good idea.

In the weeks following, I got three more messages from other DEA "agents" saying my name had come up in drug investigations. Needless to say, I did not respond.

This noxious scam became so widespread that *Nightline* covered it. In Texas, these thugs had actually sent a Suburban to park in front of the mark's house. One poor, terrified woman shot herself when she saw the SUV outside.

I like to think of myself as a fairly intelligent person. Hell, I only missed being on *Jeopardy* by two questions when I auditioned. But, I learned that I could be easily rattled. My good sense thrown out the window. Fear, threats, images of being ripped from my family, turned me from someone I believed was an urbane intellectual into a trembling, panicked idiot that was nearly taken for an expensive and embarrassing ride.

James Utt hopes the people behind this horrid crime are caught and put in jail in the Dominican Republic.

HOLIDAYS BRING
MIXED EMOTIONS

A COUPLE OF things make me uncomfortable about December. First, it gets dark way too early and second, it is a religious time of year. You see, I have lost my faith. After so many years of being a practicing Catholic, the rising waters of doubt covered the rock of my faith and agnosticism became my intellectual home.

There aren't that many of us. Agnostics are about 4 percent of the population, atheists about the same. Out of the 535 members of Congress there is not one declared atheist. There are openly gay members, a Muslim, a Hindu, but no nonbelievers. It is still a bridge too far for American voters. So, it can be lonely out here in nonbeliever land, especially during the Christmas season. Every so often, I am slightly tempted to take what the Danish philosopher Kierkegaard called "the leap of faith." But it is just too great a jump.

Sometimes it is tempting to use my agnosticism as a cudgel and swing it at Christian fanatics like Pat Robertson who claimed Hurricane Katrina was God's punishment for abortion. There is also Southern Baptist leader Robert Jeffress, a man President Trump recently described as "wonderful," who said in 2011 the Catholic Church was a cult-like religion whose success was due to "the genius of Satan." But I know these are minority voices, except maybe in Alabama.

But at age 70, I have found anger to be an unproductive emotion; even for those that tell me one of my son's souls is in danger because he is gay. There are hundreds of millions of devoted, committed Christians following the teaching of Jesus, working for social justice. I honor and admire them.

It is hard not to be moved by the warmth of our town during the holidays. The striking beauty of the bells coming from the Presbyterian Church on Forest brings me to a stop each time I hear them. The way the downtown is festooned with lights is a joyous sight. People seem to put the issues of parking, short-term rentals, and historic home designation on the back burner and concentrate on being friendlier.

We agnostics and atheists can partake in the joy of the season even though we do not believe a man from Nazareth is the messiah. I don't mean just the "eat, drink, and be merry," part, although that is not a bad ethos for any season. We can use this season as an inspiration to rededicate ourselves to spreading goodwill among those we come in contact with. We can make an extra effort to work for peace. We can work together in the spirit of Christmas to give those that have little, just a little more.

Yes, we can have a joyous, secular Christmas time.

It was being said by some that without religion, people have no moral anchor, that it is impossible to lead a good life. I disagree. All one really needs to lead a good life is to follow the Golden Rule, which was, by the way, taught by Buddha and Confucius 500 years before Jesus.

As I leave Bushards after picking up some of the many pills that help me stay around, I hear the bells coming from the nearby church. As always, I stop and listen. The sun is shining, people on Forest are smiling, and it is a good time to be alive. So, "Merry Christmas," or "Happy Holidays," or just "have a nice day."

James Utt hopes the spirit of the season will last a bit longer than a few weeks into January.

ODE TO LAGUNA BEACH

BEFORE ANYONE KNEW about the Irvine Company, everyone in Orange County knew about the Irvine Ranch. It covered one sixth of the county and, in the mid-1960s, it contained mile after mile of orange groves, sugar beets, even a herd of cattle. I worked for the ranch in the summers during high school and a year into college. There was actually a bunkhouse, where mostly old men, some of whom came out from Oklahoma during the Dust Bowl, lived for a dollar a day, room and board.

Eventually, I was entrusted with my own truck and a small crew. One day, the foreman told me to load up my truck with potted small trees and take them to a bluff that overlooked the ocean in Newport Beach. There was to be some kind of groundbreaking ceremony. As I would learn later, it was for the building of what would become Fashion Island. As I look back now, I ask myself, what had I, in some small part, wrought upon this land?

There are times when I must visit Fashion Island or other environs of Newport Beach: To visit relatives, conduct financial affairs, see an overpriced movie. When I finish my affairs and drive south, the image of Tim Robbins' character escaping the Shawshank State Prison often comes into my mind.

First, one must escape the seemingly benign claws of Corona del

Mar, which has a touch, just a touch, of Laguna's community feel. Soon, I can see the ocean from PCH, which means I will shortly have to run the gauntlet of the monster homes above Crystal Cove. Remember when there was nothing on those hills? It was a scenic buffer zone between Newport and Laguna. Now look at it. One of the saddest sights of the journey south is the "new" Javier's. Longtime residents of Laguna Beach can recall the "old" Javier's, across from the Hotel Laguna. Its casual intimacy, the people lined up and chatting as they waited for a table, the small bar where people relaxed with a beer as they watched a game. Want a feel for the new place? Go there on a Thursday night, rent yourself a Porsche for the valet, borrow some Armani and sit in the cavernous bar and watch what unfolds. Nothing epitomizes the difference between Laguna Beach and Newport more than this place.

El Morro Elementary School. Almost home. When I reach the two stoplights by the Shell station, the same good feeling comes over me as when I drive through the canyon and go past the Sawdust grounds. I am back in Laguna Beach. The pull of the Husky Boy Burgers is strong, but I am going to eat healthy tonight, maybe pizza. Then comes Boat Canyon with my UPS, dry cleaners, Gina's. Turn right on Myrtle and stop along Heisler Park, where you can see, smell, almost feel the ocean. But it is crowded with visitors. When my wife and I moved to Laguna, there was actually an "off season."

Is it wrong or selfish of me to wish that the tide of tourists receded for some months of the year? That we locals experience the intimacy of a less crowded village for a few precious weeks?

Turn back on to PCH going south and there is Main Beach, the boardwalk, and the classic lifeguard tower. On the grass that separates the street from the beach there are often people with signs making political statements. Sometimes I honk in support. There are also the homeless. They are treated far better here than most cities as they struggle to hold on to the shreds of dignity they still possess.

Now I pass Legion to Cleo where I turn in to Ralphs. Pete the cat needs some food. I could use some Scotch. The parking lot is too small, the aisles are too narrow, but they have the friendliest checkers in the world.

At home, Pete fed, drink in hand, music playing, I can look down, not on Fashion Island or a flotilla of yachts, but on the town that is my home.

James Utt is a retired social science teacher who has lived in Laguna Beach since 2001. He actually has some friends who live in Newport. They would like to move to Laguna Beach.

PART THREE
SCENES OF MY LAGUNA

Jane Hanauer at Laguna Beach Books, a local literary treasure.

Pacific Coast Highway at rest.

So many disappointments, maybe this will be the year.

Age and injuries keep me away from here.

Jack the Cat's bathroom revenge.

Why look at the ocean when you can look at your phone?

The people that keep me alive at Bushards Pharmacy.

The Lonely Laguna Beach Theater

The Brooks Street Sidewalk Surfer

The Beauty of Crescent Bay

Let her not be forgotten.

PART FOUR
BOOMER WAILS

ALONE, BUT WARMED BY
MY ADOPTED HOMETOWN

In 2001, OUR children out of high school, my wife convinced me we should move to Laguna, the city where she had grown up. Reluctant at first to leave Irvine, our home of 20 years, I was soon seduced by the beauty, warmth, and charm of this city. Moving from the sterile planned community of Irvine to Laguna was like that part in the *Wizard of Oz* where the picture changes from black-and-white to color.

And there is no more wonderful time of year in this city than the holiday season. The beautiful antique street lamps, the trees around the village festooned with lights, the trollies driven by, perhaps, the real Santa himself—top all this off with the gentle beauty of the sounds of the bells from the Presbyterian Church, as if Quasimodo himself was ringing them to call the residents of Paris to Mass—who could not be moved by all of this?

Yet, I cannot be moved in the same way that most are by the spirit of the season because I am an agnostic. Try as I might, and I tried for many years, I cannot believe in what I see as a lovely fabrication. If I could believe it would be a soothing balm for my wounded heart. On July 14 of last year, while the French were celebrating Bastille Day, cancer was busy wringing the last few ounces of life from my wife's tortured body. Well-meaning people tell me my wife "is in a better place." Not unless being in an urn at the bottom of the sea just off our coast is better than living on Tahiti Avenue with a husband that loves you. There are times when I am envious of those who are so comfortable, so reassured by their faith, yet I am unable to take what the philosopher Kierkegaard called "the leap of faith." It's just too far to jump.

Before my wife became too ill to travel, we spent many holiday seasons in Manhattan and we loved to walk the streets at night. Lexington Avenue, Broadway, 5th Avenue, all were breathtaking in their energy and excitement. We loved our time there. However, our favorite holiday street remained Forest Avenue here in Laguna because it was our home. New Yorkers get a bad rap for being brusque or haughty. Some are, most aren't. But the friendliness that seems to be endemic to the residents of Laguna wins my heart hands down over any place we had traveled to in our 39 years together.

A couple of years ago, when my wife was still able to walk medium distances, we strolled hand in hand from City Hall, down Forest and back up Ocean, surrounded by smiling faces of residents and tourists alike. We wished we could somehow capture the spirit of the holiday season and spread it around the rest of the year. The country, indeed the world, could use a little more joy and a lot more peace on earth.

This past Christmas, the first after Kathy's death, I did not walk the streets during the holiday season. It would be too lonely, I thought. This year I plan to resume the walk. I will probably start at the new senior center, because, well, dear god—agnostics can still use this term—I am now a senior. I will walk toward City Hall, passing under the wonderful street lamps, see the huge tree lit in front of City Hall and then turn down Forest. I won't stop in at the Lumberyard, which was Cedar Creek when we moved here, because the last time Kathy and I ate out, it was there. Still can't go back.

Across the street from Lumberyard is Stephen Frank, Kathy's favorite shop in all of Laguna, run by the most warm and helpful people I have met in this town. I will stop in and say hello. Then across Forest to the Flower Stand, run by Bev, a native of South Africa and simply a wonderful person. It is here I buy Kathy's favorite flowers to place in our house to remind me of the fragrances she loved so much. A few yards further down Forest to Rock Martin where Michael and Heather made such beautiful jewelry for Kathy for those special occasions like birthdays and anniversaries. I will forever be grateful to them. Bushards will probably be closed but I will think of their most helpful staff as I go by. I never fail to feel better after a visit with the good people who work there. Their smiles and friendly attitudes are as valuable as the drugs they dispense. A few quick steps further down Forest and I am at 230, where at *least* one drink must be consumed. Over the years it has been my *Cheers*, sharing drinks and conversation with dear friends, one in particular, who have helped to keep me afloat during the stressful times. Laughter and thoughtful conversation does help to keep the darkness at bay.

No, I do not believe in the Christmas story, but the warmth of Laguna and its residents during this holiday season helps to fill a hole in my heart and, just maybe, my soul.

James Utt is a retired high school teacher who enjoys, reading, travel, tennis, and Scotch. Not necessarily in that order.

A FIGHT WELL FOUGHT,
A WIFE REMEMBERED

SOUTHERN CALIFORNIA EDISON had a scheduled power outage that was running hours past the time they said it would be over. My wife and I sat talking by candlelight sipping wine and nearly running out of things to say. Finally, the power came back on and we noticed the flashing red signal on our landline that told us we had a voicemail. It had, of course, been left several hours earlier and was from the oncologist.

My wife's first mastectomy was in 2000 and was a huge success, with a marvelous reconstruction and five years of Tamoxifen as a precaution. We moved to Laguna Beach and life was good. For a while. In 2009, cancer was discovered in her other breast, another mastectomy and a not-so-good reconstruction. We both found it harder to bounce back from this one. Lots of chemo at that dreary place on Old Newport Road where 20 other people were hooked up to drips. After a period of time the doctor gave us a cautious all clear and we tried to resume a normal life.

But not two years later, we learned that apparently a tiny part of the cancer had escaped and found a home on my wife's liver. More chemo and, when the cancer had decreased in size enough, a procedure called an ablation, to effectively destroy it. This, too, was deemed a success. The third time was the charm. Only it wasn't, as the late-night message told us. The cancer that refused to die was back and it was serious.

More and different chemo drugs were dripped into her in five-hour sessions. She researched each one and learned that these were last-ditch efforts, despite our oncologist's reassurance that "we've had great success with this one." My wife battled on in a braver fashion than I could ever imagine myself doing under similar circumstances. She continued to work full-time even though her pain was often excruciating, eschewing medical marijuana for the medical martini.

We would watch television with our drinks until she became sleepy and then turn in. One night she said, "I can't stand up." More desperate treatments, more trips to the hospital, and a growing pessimism from our doctor. The wheelchair made its appearance. And finally, the oncologist said what we both knew he would say. "We have to concentrate on your comfort now because there is nothing more we can do to stop your decline. I am very sorry." His staff would arrange for hospice people to contact us at once. He told my wife she had between four and six months to live.

She died in three weeks. If the hospice people had the power to keep someone alive, my wife would have lived forever. They were the kindest, most helpful, and supportive people I have ever come in contact with, but even they could not arrest her decline. A hospital bed she could never get comfortable in, searing pain that morphine could not dampen, humiliating failures to get to the toilet in time. I would like to think that those last three weeks brought us closer together, as the past few years had seemed to drive a wedge between us. I hope so, but I will never know.

As the French were celebrating Bastille Day on July 14th, some nice people from McCormick & Son Mortuaries came and took my wife's body away, her suffering over. The last I saw of the woman I had shared nearly 40 years of my life with was her body wrapped in a sheet, being taken to a waiting van. It has been said before that you don't know what you've got until it's gone.

Sometimes, late at night, I put on just a little of my wife's perfume, and try to recapture a small slice of our life together.

If James Utt has a soul, there would be a hole in it since his wife's death.

AGAIN IN TEN YEARS, MAYBE

Besides hordes of tourists coming to Southern California beach communities, do you know who else descends on us in huge numbers? Dry-wood termites, that's who, and sometimes they bring along their pals, subterranean termites. We've all seen a home that all of a sudden is enclosed in a multi-colored tent. Oh, the hassle, the cost. Those poor people.

As I understand, the rule is that one should tent their home every ten years. We bought our home in 2001 and it has been untented ever since. Nope, not going to do it; I would be among "the untented."

My contractor tells me he sees signs of termite damage under my deck. Okay, but he replaced that wood. No problem. During the hot months, a swarm of termites comes up from a floor vent. But it will get cooler soon and they will hibernate. They do hibernate, don't they? I pull back the covers on my bed and there is a termite. But I had just changed the sheets and maybe he just wants a good night's sleep. He doesn't snore and I am not made of wood. Again, no problem.

But I could not ignore the actual termite inspector who thoroughly checked my entire house and found plenty of dry-wood termites and warned the hillside was a prime target for the much more dangerous "subs." The subterranean guys could be taken of care by drilling bait stations around the house. When it came to the dry-wood termites, there was only one remedy—the much dreaded and delayed tenting.

Tenting your house is kind of like a colonoscopy. The prep is the worst part. The carefully nurtured ivy and ice plant that grew on the walls of my deck had to be brutally cut back to make room for the sand bags that would hold the tent down. Almost every type of food, even inside the fridge, had to be double bagged. Being now a widower, I did not have that much food and tried to eat out as much as possible leading up to the day of the tenting. My wife must have had a hundred spices in the cupboard and I checked the "use by" date on each one. No, that's not true. I just started throwing ones out I never used.

My two aging cats had to be put in their carriers and boarded at the animal hospital. They have been to the vet so many times, they seem to see something in my eyes that tells them, "He's going to put us in those cages again." They do not go willingly. I am on blood thinners and by the time I get them into the car, it looks like I have lost a fight with an angry rosebush. We inherited a fish tank that came with the house and since the gas would kill the fish—I was tempted—they had to be transported to a fish hostel by the guy that maintains the tank.

Of course, lodging had to be found for two nights and three days and I decided to stay in town. Any hotel would be fine; it's Laguna after all. Well, not quite. My assigned room faced PCH and I received a taste of what it must be like to be at the Indianapolis 500. When I tried to use the bathroom, the door hit the toilet seat instead of opening all the way. At night, sleep would not come because my mind dwelt on the stories told to me about how gangs use gas masks and go into tented homes. The next morning, after a few hours of restless sleep, I had breakfast downstairs and it might have been tasty if it was hot. I would have even settled for warm.

But, the ordeal came to an end. The tenting was removed and I escaped my hotel. However, the termites were not the only casualties.

My late wife loved indoor plants and our house was filled with beautiful greenery. I had been doing a pretty good job keeping them alive. Until now. Because I am an idiot, I thought that indoor plants were hardy enough to take two days' worth of direct April sun, so out on the front lawn they went. They all ended up dying. Another small part of my wife had been lost.

Termite wise, the house is good for another ten years. If still alive, rather than go through this again, I just might say to the termites, "Okay, show me what you got!"

James Utt is a retired teacher who lives temporarily termite free in Mystic Hills.

IOWA? NEW HAMPSHIRE?
WHY NOT LAGUNA BEACH?

EVERY FOUR YEARS as I sit here in California, I am gripped by a sense of powerlessness and frustration. First the Iowa caucus, then the New Hampshire primary take place and they go a long way, a long disproportional way, toward determining whom the presidential candidates will be. Look, New Hampshire is a beautiful state and my very best friend is from there, but come on. Candidates spend so much time there they have met every prospective voter twice. Be a sitting president who loses or does poorly in this little giant and you might very well drop out of the race. Ask Truman or LBJ. Is this state that representative of our nation that it should be granted so much political influence?

And the Iowa caucus? Only a small percentage of eligible voters brave the January weather to often spend hours selecting their delegates. Those that show up tend to be the "base" of the party, people who are more likely to support candidates on the ideological boundaries like Rick Santorum in 2012. It is difficult for independents to take part in the caucuses, and the evangelical Christians turn out at twice the rate of their actual population in the state. Iowa is also the state that has the lowest percentage of businesses owned by women.

And they really stunk up the Rose Bowl this year. Should this be a bellwether state?

Both of these states are far more rural than the US as a whole. Iowa is 36 percent rural, New Hampshire nearly 40 percent, while the nation as a whole is about 19 percent. We need a better starting point for the presidential selection process and I believe I have one, although it would call upon the citizens of our city to put up with a great deal.

That's right. I propose that the first presidential primary should be held in Laguna Beach!

There would be a time limit on how long candidates could actually campaign here though. Instead of the two-year dating period wannabe presidents have with Iowa and New Hampshire, I suggest we limit campaigning here to one month. And that would be February, the shortest month.

But wait you say, aren't we too … untypical a city for this task? Not at all. Despite our liberal reputation, political party affiliation is about equally divided. We are not Newport Beach. Some of you might say, "Well, aren't we a little too racially homogeneous for this task?" It is true that Laguna is 90 percent white, but Iowa is 92 percent white, and New Hampshire 94 percent. So what's the big deal there? And, in our fair city, women own 30 percent of businesses. Add to this the fact that 65 percent of folks here have at least a Bachelor of Arts degree, compared with Iowa's 25 percent and New Hampshire's 36 percent, and I think we're looking pretty darn good as the site of the first primary. We are smart, open-minded, tolerant, hey, we've even got churches and lawn bowling.

And think of the advantages for the candidates themselves. Instead of having to attend the Iowa State Fair, and dine on dishes that could be called "heart attacks on a plate," they could sample some of the best and most unique restaurants in the state. And they would not have to talk about ethanol. Instead of tramping through the snows of New Hampshire, they could campaign in the mild, sunny climate that we usually experience in February. The danger is that some of the candidates might like it here so much they might stop campaigning and become residents who start their own businesses. Imagine "Pantsuits by Hillary," "Christie's Real Jersey Pizza," "The Donald Hair Salon."

Yes, we residents of the city would have to put up with intrusions. Big buses, the press everywhere, traffic snarls, being interrupted at our favorite restaurants by candidate "drop-ins," but I think we would take one for the team, so to speak, to get the election cycle off to a decent start.

Plato believed that democracy would not work because the average citizen was not informed enough, not smart enough, not involved enough to make intelligent choices. Plato was never in Laguna Beach.

James Utt believes that our country takes too long to nominate a presidential candidate and, even then, we end up with weak choices.

SAY IT AIN'T SO, A VALENTINE'S STORY

WHEN IT BECAME known that the legendary Bob Dylan was going to do a television commercial for IBM, my first reaction was, "Say it ain't so, Bob, say it ain't so." One of my favorite adages from the Black Sox scandal of 1919. Bob Dylan doing a TV ad for IBM? This struck me as incongruous and disappointing in the extreme. Would Gandhi have done plugs for Bollywood films? Would Jackson Pollock have done a joint exhibit with Norman Rockwell? What's next, seeing Golden Arches on our beautiful boardwalk? How about a garish new Trump Tower next to the iconic Hotel Laguna?

More disturbing than Dylan shilling for IBM was what he admitted in the commercial that his main themes were, "Time passes and love fades." Bob, what about "Wedding Song," "She Belongs to Me," "Sad Eyed Lady of the Lowlands?" Let us Laguna Beach romantics have our dreams of undying love.

I know, I know, you don't have to look far to see that there is some truth in Dylan's view that love is transitory. One out of every two marriages fails in this country. I know couples that have stayed together "for the kids." Even sadder are couples I know who, over the years, have become people who share the same address, but not the same heart, roommates rather than lovers.

For most of my life, I have been a cynic, a skeptic when it came to things like organized religion or humankind's ability to avoid wars, brutality, and inhumanity. Devotion to our gods, over-identification with our own nations, our own ethnic groups—look where that has brought us today. Our world is one bleak, scarred place. That is why I cannot accept Dylan's proposition about love. There must be the hope that there is something we can hold on to, something that lasts, something that does not fade.

Love can be the most reliable and sustaining feature of human existence. Returning to Gandhi, he said, "Where there is love, there is life." Whether it is the sensual love of Eros or the selfless love of agape, loving another person truly, completely, and having that love returned to you, is the greatest thing we can hope for as we stroll across the stage that is our short lives. I walk hand in hand with another and I am richer, stronger for it.

Without a belief that love is lasting, durable, capable of dealing with life's adversities, we are ships sailing aimlessly across the seas, finding only fleeting pleasure in the harbors that in the light of day turn cold. Oscar Wilde, who suffered much for love, said, "Keep love in your heart. A life without it is like a sunless garden when the flowers are dead."

Since Bob Dylan is a songwriter, let me answer his belief that love fades with the words of another songwriter, John Deacon from the band Queen. In the song "You're My Best Friend," he wrote these words to his wife, "Oh, you're my best friend that I've ever had, I've been with you such a long time, You're my sunshine and I want you to know, that my feelings are true, I really love you, Oh, you're my best friend."

Bob, love need not fade. I think you got that one wrong.

James Utt believes that if we have lost Bob Dylan to High Tech we are really in a world of hurt.

READ WIDELY, BUY LOCALLY

I HAVE DONE it; most likely you have, too. It is so easy. Maybe you've heard about a book that sounds interesting and you find it on Amazon, read some reviews by people who are often paid to give their opinions, and with one click you have bought the book and it will be delivered to your door. Or perhaps you have been seduced by the size of a Barnes & Noble. Bigger must be better, right? In you go, wander around, searching, waiting for a friendly face to give you some attention and assistance, and you often wait in vain.

Those of us concerned about this issue might be fighting a rear-guard action against forces that cannot be stopped. But we must be willing to go down swinging, because we as a nation are on the verge of losing a precious resource: the local bookstore.

I recently spoke with Jane Hanauer, the proprietor of Laguna Beach Books, who alerted me to some alarming trends. When they opened in 2006, there were 6000 independent local bookstores across the nation. Today there are 2000. This mirrors Laguna's decline from three bookstores, when my wife and I moved here in 2001, to just one today. But it is a magnificent one, as are so many fighting to stay afloat in today's online, big box store world.

Growing up in Santa Ana in the 1950s my mother or grand-mother would often take me to a small bookstore on Fourth Street.

I remember the warm smile of the owner when we walked in as a small bell attached to the door tingled. There was no rush, we could touch, browse, and sit down with our books. Looking back, since it was Santa Ana in the '50s, there seemed to be a lot of books on the dangers of communism, like *The Naked Communist.* There was also a hearty supply of books on the power of religion and positive thinking. Oh, well, that was then. I was too young to realize it, but small bookstores gave us a sense of community. I always felt a sense of warmth and welcome from the husband and wife who ran the store. Is it too much of a dream to think we can recapture just a little of those feelings as we shop today?

The great writer Ann Patchett says local bookstores are "a place to raise up readers." Ms. Hanauer proudly points out that 25 percent of their sales are children or young adult titles. As a former teacher, I cannot tell you how important it is to engage children in reading as soon as possible. And I don't mean on a Kindle!

A few more words about Laguna Beach Books, and local bookstores in general. They are so much more than sellers of books. They have open mic nights, poetry readings, book clubs, and authors, both locally and nationally known. Not so long ago I had the pleasure of meeting T. Jefferson Parker, whose *Laguna Heat* remains one of my favorite books, at Laguna Beach Books. We both lived in Tustin and went to Tustin High and both had the good sense to flee to Laguna Beach, where the view is better, the air is fresher, and the smell of Birch is much less evident.

When I asked Ms. Hanauer why she believed local bookstores are crucial, she replied, "They help to define the town." Count me among those who want to help define Laguna Beach as something special, rather than help the tightfisted Jeff Bezos get yet more money.

As I concluded my talk with Ms. Hanauer, I walked from the back room toward the front door, passing the 20,000 titles, seeing mothers with young children, and seeing a customer with two large, well behaved dogs laying at her feet. Everyone was being helped by smiling employees.

So, it may be easier to buy on Amazon with one click, but you are missing a great deal. Leave Laguna Beach Books and turn left and you can buy vinyl from Sound Spectrum, turn right and visit a dozen shops or dine at Sapphire, maybe even talk to the spinning guy at the corner of PCH and Brooks, one of the nicest residents of our town.

What makes Laguna Beach special is that we are a community. We are not our neighbors to the north. Let's support our community, and communities like ours, by buying books locally.

James Utt is an avid reader who does not use Amazon to buy books.

SEMI TOUGH ISN'T ENOUGH

My THERAPIST SAYS dwelling on mistakes made in the past serves no useful purpose. Learn from them and move on. But I am a stubborn client. Since June is Gay Pride Month, I find myself thinking often about an incident that happened years ago at the corner of PCH and Cress, and how I could have dealt with it better.

My wife and I had just finished drinks at the Rooftop Lounge, where once again I was the oldest person there. Can't there be a bar in town where you have to show your AARP card to gain entry? We were waiting for the light to change to cross PCH when we noticed a car next to us that was also waiting for a green light. There were two men next to us. They might have been gay. Who could know for sure, and more importantly, who should care? These two caught the eye of the driver who leaned out the window and, trying to affect an effeminate voice, said, "Hey, boys, which way to Woody's?" Both men in the car laughed heartily.

A couple of things occurred to me. If he knew anything about Laguna Beach, he would have been aware that Woody's, Laguna's beloved gay bar, was now a Mexican restaurant just to his right. The other thing that instantly came to mind was that I have a gay son. I would not let these guys get away with this behavior.

I took my wife by the hand and stepped in front of the possibly gay couple and yelled at the car, "Hey, jerk, you're in the wrong city. Go back to San Bernardino with the rest of the rednecks!" The light changed, and they sped through the crosswalk, pedestrians be damned. As they fled, they gave me the one finger salute.

In retrospect I should have done several things differently. First, calling him a "jerk" could have resulted in the driver getting out of the car and pounding my 60-something body into the sidewalk. I could have also been more articulate and said, "That's not nearly as funny as you seem to think," or "Are you so hard up for fun that you have to insult people?"

Another thing I should not have done was insult San Bernardino. They had stereotyped Laguna Beach as full of gays. I suggested that the Inland Empire was homophobic and redneck. For all I knew, those guys could have lived in Dana Point. Even in this time of increasing tolerance, there is antigay sentiment in many parts of the soft underbelly of our country. It is not confined to one city, state, or region.

But my biggest regret is that I acted cowardly, even though I did take the risk of being beaten up by the Westboro Baptist Church boys, secular division. When my wife and I crossed the street she asked, "Why did you take my hand when you stepped in front of the gay guys? Since I was in heels, did you think my tall stature would intimidate them?"

We both knew the answer. I wanted to make sure the two in the car knew I was a straight guy with a good-looking woman by his side. More courageous would have been to step out by myself and confront these bullies. Let them think me gay. I should not have used my wife as a heterosexual prop in confronting these ill-mannered visitors to our city. I could have even put my hand on the shoulder of one of the men next to me and said to the driver, "We don't appreciate bigotry here in Laguna. Just be on your way."

Yes, in a way, I had acted tough, but really only semi-tough. I felt I needed my wife as my wing person, so to speak, when a braver behavior would have been to act solo.

We don't get chances to be heroic that often. I hope I get another chance.

James Utt is a sixteen-year resident of Laguna Beach. He wishes Woody's and the Boom were still around.

A LUDDITE'S LAMENT

I HEARD A story at a brunch that I should have been shocked by, but sadly was not. An acquaintance was walking along Heisler Park and spied a blue whale remarkably close to shore. He excitedly shouted to the person next to him to take notice of this magnificent sight. This happened to be a young man who had his face buried in his tablet and, without looking up, said, "I'll catch it on YouTube."

Warming up for a doubles match at beautiful Alta Laguna Park last fall, I noticed that the guy I was hitting to was on his cell phone. Guess he was a good multitasker or he didn't need much concentration to keep the ball in play against me.

Not so long ago, my date and I joined another couple at one of Laguna's more trendy restaurants near Forest and Glenneyre. I knew it had to be trendy because I was the oldest person there. When seated, we could not help notice that several young couples were not talking to each other but had their eyes glued to their cell phones.

Signs and wonders.

Would it be too much to ask that our community use social media less? That we actually speak in real time with other people? That we live a bit less plugged in? I do think it would fit in more with who we are and who we have been as a community.

It is lonely out here in anti-social media land. I am told I am being a cranky old guy, missing out on so much, in danger of being left behind. The guy you warn your Thanksgiving guests about. "Watch out for Uncle Jim. After a couple of drinks, he'll go off on Facebook or Kindles. Just try and get him back into the football game or get him another Scotch."

True, I am the only person I know who is not on Facebook. Own a Kindle? Please. Amazon recently sent out an email stating that books would soon go the way of the rotary phone. I think that would be a loss of immeasurable proportions. Books are to be held, looked at, given as gifts the receiver can see, touch, or even write in. "Hey, I just bought you *To Kill a Mockingbird*, Kindle edition." I think not.

Twitter, Instagram? Aren't there other things we could be doing, especially in our fair town, instead of retreating to these? Last season, the University of Michigan lost a game on the last play because their punter fumbled a snap. Thanks to Twitter, he was getting death threats within the hour. What a big step forward for human communication.

Americans spend an average of five hours a day with digital media, more than half of that time on mobile devices. According to a UK study we check our phones 221 times a day. It seems we are headed for a time where not being a participant in social media would indicate either eccentricity, social marginalization, or old age.

Dr. Sherry Turkle of MIT has been researching the effects of the overuse of social media on Americans. She has found that the new communications revolution is degrading the quality of relationships. Professors gaze out at a room full of semi-engaged multitaskers. In the online dating world of infinite choices, it is more difficult for emotional commitments. Most alarming of all is that young people are not learning how to be alone. "It is the capacity for solitude that allows you to reach out to others and see them as separate and independent," she writes.

I fear we are beginning to lose the most human thing we do and that is to have face-to-face conversations.

Back to that trendy restaurant I spoke of earlier. Even though I am a baby boomer, my date was a much younger woman. Must have been my fame as a writer, which has spread from one end of Third Street all the way to the other, that got her attention. After what I thought was a fairly intimate dinner, I envisioned further plans for the evening. As we were walking toward my car, her cell phone rang.

"Oh, it's my friend Krista. I've got to see what she's up to." She was still speaking on her cell as I opened the car door, still totally engrossed in her conservation. I had a sexual insurance policy in my pocket, an ED pill—hey, even Luddites can use pharmaceuticals—but I now had no desire other than to take her straight home and say goodnight.

James Utt is a retired social science teacher who has lived in Laguna Beach since 2001. He misses his chalk and blackboard.

MEET, NOT MEAT

I HAVE LIVED in Laguna Beach since 2001, though many old-time residents still consider me new to town. I have tried hard to become a part of the place my heart has embraced. Purchasing things from local artists, taking classes at the Susi Q. Center, reading at open mic sessions at Laguna Beach Books, making friends with several local bartenders—all these things I have done and more. My name appears among the founders of the Third Street Writers and my columns run in the *Laguna Beach Independent*.

But there is one quintessential Laguna experience I have shied away from: dining at Zinc Cafe. Zinc prides itself in serving healthy fare, and my diet is, shall we say, one that does not encourage longevity.

I still grieve the closing of the Jolly Roger on PCH where one could unselfconsciously bathe hash browns in ketchup and devour bacon or sausage or both. Had I been born a dinosaur, I would not have been a leaf-eating stegosaurus but a meat-seeking T-Rex. I did try to be a vegetarian once after reading a book that described the horrid conditions of factory farms, but as it says in Matthew, "The spirit was willing but the flesh was weak." If the Animal Liberation Front is correct when they say, "Meat is Murder," then I am long overdue for a cell on death row. Feed me a steady diet of vegetables, withhold from me my M and M's, deny me nature's most perfect food, the Cheetos, and I would consider these, to use Dick Cheney's phrase, "enhanced interrogation techniques."

And there stands Zinc, meatless Zinc. I had been there one time with a friend for a quick bite, but I was more interested in her and did not absorb the Zinc experience. I have walked by the place on numerous occasions and, letting my imagination run wild, have seen people sitting at the tables who brought to mind those who frequented French salons in the Enlightenment. These were the people who probably knew the working of the city council, had their finger on the pulse of the art scene, read books by Jonathan Franzen or Ann Patchett. Even their dogs were well behaved.

Deciding to return, I did a scouting trip early one morning and glanced at the menu. Under "hot drinks" it had a list of "Intelligentsia Coffee." Oh no, are they openly catering to the "intelligentsia" of Laguna, that social class of people guiding, critiquing, or shaping culture and politics? That seemed a bit much. Then I learned that Intelligentsia Coffee is a special brand that is handcrafted for coffee aficionados. Okay, but still I wonder if these beans are any better than the coffee I had at truck stops when I would accompany my father on his long hauls to Canada?

Next, a decision had to be made as to what reading material to bring to this unique spot. Simply gazing out at Ocean Avenue or, for this Luddite, bringing an electronic device was unacceptable. The *Register* was a nonstarter, the *Los Angeles Times* a possibility. I could go really intelligentsia on them and bring a copy of the *New York Review of Books*, or try for the local angle and bring a copy of the *Indy*. I finally decided to bring a notebook, in which people might think I was writing poetry, when in truth, it was being used to take notes.

The day arrived and I had lunch at Zinc. The staff was extremely friendly and the quesadilla plate was delicious. I noticed that some people came in large groups and others ran into people they knew and sat down at their tables and engaged in real conversation. There was laughter. There was camaraderie. But no place is perfect, and there were a few patrons who looked at cell phones instead of each other. When I strained to eavesdrop, I heard interesting bits of conversation about politics, both local and national, about upcoming art events, and travel trips recently completed. It was an Enlightenment salon with a dash of social media.

Strolling up Ocean Avenue, I felt more a part of my town. I knew I would return again some day. As soon as they add a French dip sandwich to their menu.

James Utt is a retired high school teacher who has lived in Laguna Beach for sixteen years. He has never had a latte.

THE PRICE OF PARADISE

THE SUMMER HAS arrived and the much-ballyhooed El Nino seems to have made about as much of an impression on us as Jeb Bush's presidential campaign. Think back several months to the sizzling October we endured when we longed for El Nino's early arrival. I remember a day in that hot month that I will not soon forget. The air-conditioning unit was fighting a valiant, but losing, battle to keep the house temperature at a tolerable level. The many large glass windows, which gave such a beautiful view of the city below and the ocean beyond, were giving me a practical lesson in the Greenhouse Effect.

Having retreated to a cooler back bedroom with whatever book I was reading at the time, there was suddenly a loud snap, or crackle, or pop. One of the aging cats must have knocked something over. Again. Going through the house, finding nothing broken, my puzzlement increased until I looked out and saw a shattered glass pane, one of several that enclosed my deck. Had someone fired a pellet gun in the direction of my home? Unlikely. Could a very large bird have become disoriented by the heat and flown into it? Again, unlikely, unless pterodactyls have made a comeback. A hurried call to my reliable contractor cleared things up. Heat causes things to expand, and with it anchored in stucco on the bottom, and by a tube on the top, the glass simply could not help itself. It was forced to shatter.

I walked out on the deck and looked past the glass to the bone-dry landscape below. My house is in Mystic Hills on one of the streets so devastated by the 1993 fire. We did not live here then, but when we bought the rebuild home in 2001, the previous owners left us a ghostly picture of them standing by the fireplace, pretty much all that remained after that horrific evening. We were assured that it was much safer to live in this area now: stricter building codes, more water available for the fire department, even a herd of goats to eat, well, practically anything that grew on the hillside.

My wife and I truly enjoyed the sights and sounds of the herd when they were below our home, even if the shepherd used the hose on our slope without asking, to provide water to his hundred or more goats. He had a dog; it must have been a border collie. This clever animal kept the herd disciplined when they had to be moved, just like a drill sergeant maneuvers new recruits in basic training. But I have not seen the herd below my home in a long time. Is it because the lack of rain has left them nothing to devour? When will it rain again? I miss the goats, I miss the dog, I even miss the shepherd who used my water and asked my next-door neighbor if he could use his phone to make just one call. When my neighbor received his phone bill, he saw that the man had called someone in South America.

Gone also is my wife, who passed away three years ago, and my sons who have moved away. Living alone has but a few perks: mixing colors with whites on laundry day, being able to watch too much football, not having to eat Brussels sprouts. But it also brings an emptiness that wraps itself around me like a blanket that gives no heat. There is no one to talk to when conversation is so necessary to combat loneliness. No one to rant to when I have just seen an idiot flip a cigarette out of the window of his car as he drove through the canyon with red fire warning flags all around. No one to soothe my fears when the winds of October and November come calling, when one spark could ignite our hillsides, forcing me to make the terrible decision: what things do I take with me as I evacuate?

Again, I look past the shattered glass and down my slope at the city below. I am reminded that Laguna Beach is a marvelous place to live, with its beauty, charm, sense of community—all make it like no other city in Orange County. But, because of its hilly topography and wild lands, it is subject to fires, floods, and landslides. I struggle to remind myself that every paradise has its price, and, in the end, I will gladly pay Laguna's price.

James Utt is a retired social science teacher who has lived in Laguna Beach since 2001. He hates the Santa Ana winds.

THE ANGST OF AN
ANGEL FAN

I WOULD LIKE to offer a belated congratulations to the Laguna Beach High baseball team for winning the CIF title this spring. It is a great accomplishment for their program, the school, and our city.

Their success has helped ease my pain, as I suffer through another year of seeing my beloved Angels stagger towards last place. Oh, the pain, the frustration, the heartache of so many disappointing seasons.

The Los Angeles Angels came into existence in 1961, playing their first season in a minor league park called Wrigley Field. That first year, I saw them play the Yankees when New York had Yogi Berra, Mickey Mantle, and Whitey Ford. I have lived and died with them since that game, no matter what they called themselves: The Los Angeles Angels, the California Angels, the Anaheim Angels, and now, the Los Angeles Angels of Anaheim. They were the little team in the region, never seeming to escape the shadow of their cross-town rival, the storied Dodgers.

The years from 1961 to 1978 were barren of any postseason appearances. But each winter, I would wait until spring training thinking that this would be the year. Then in 1979, they made the playoffs. And then lost to Baltimore. Three years later they were back, this time against Milwaukee. I watched the game from Hoag Hospital, where my second son had just been born. The Angels lost the deciding fifth game of the playoff series, after they had been ahead two games to none.

In 1986 came the knife to the heart. Playing the Red Sox up three games to one in the series, they were one out, one strike away from going to their first World Series. Dave Henderson hit a home run and Boston went on to win the game and the series.

Fifteen years of wandering in baseball mediocrity followed. Then, like the Israelites coming out of the desert and finding the promised land, came 2002, and a World Series victory over the Giants. Thank you Scott Spiezio for your dramatic home run! My wife was hardly a sports fan, but even she cried as the Angels hung on to win game seven.

The Angels continued to play well in the early years of this century, making the playoffs several times. But usually waiting for them in the first round were the Red Sox. The Angels were like Ahab, Boston, the White Whale. We sought them, we found them, they destroyed us.

Oh, to lose to Boston. Hey, don't get me wrong, it is a great city, an historic city, and the people showed their resilience after the marathon bombing. And who could not love "Big Papi?" I am old enough to remember that they were the last team in the majors to use black players, and the legendary Jackie Robinson said of their storied owner, Tom Yawkey, that he was "one of the most bigoted guys in baseball." The Sox fans that come to the Big A can be rather smug as they cheer on their team as they pound our poor Angels. I have asked several women I know who have worked in sports bars, "What team has the most obnoxious fans?" Universal answer: Red Sox fans. And remember, New York has baseball teams, too.

The most recent Angel seasons have been disappointing in the extreme, with the exception of the magnificent Mike Trout. Bad trades—see Wells, Vernon—and horrible free agent signings—see Hamilton, Josh—and key injuries have plagued them. This season, in particular, has been pain inducing. But I still watch, live and die with each win or loss. And after this dismal season, I shall await spring training as eagerly as a young child waits for Santa on Christmas Eve.

Even if the Angels never make it back to the World Series, I am reminded of what Bogart said to Ingrid Bergman in *Casablanca*, "We'll always have Paris." And we Angel fans will always have 2002.

So, go Angels and go Breakers baseball! Even though I am pretty sure the Breakers will make it back to the playoffs before the Angels, I am already awaiting the 2017 season.

James Utt is a retired high school teacher. He admits he sees parallels between the Angels and Sisyphus.

PUTIN'S O.C. PAL

MARCH IS JUST around the corner. As one who taught history for many years, I often think of the Ides of March, the day when Julius Caesar met his end. Popular with the masses, Caesar successfully extended the boundaries of Rome through brutal conquest and arranged to be proclaimed a dictator for life. It is no great stretch of the imagination to see parallels between Caesar and Vladimir Putin, though I don't think Caesar was seen shirtless quite as often as Czar Vlad.

Putin's past speaks for itself. He is a thug, a tyrant, and if Senator Marco Rubio is correct, which I believe he is, a war criminal. In the old Soviet Union, he was a KGB agent. What a résumé builder.

During his tenure as leader of a resurgent Russia, he has annexed Crimea, supported pro-Russian terrorists in eastern Ukraine, and engaged in a savage war in Syria in support of the murderous President Assad. The actions of his troops in Syria caused America's ambassador to the United Nations, Samantha Power, to ask her Russian counterpart, "Is there no act of barbarism against civilians, no execution of a child that gets under your skin?"

Within Russia, democratic voices, journalists, and opposition leaders have been killed under mysterious circumstances. Freedom House, a US-based nonpartisan organization that researches political freedom and human rights around the globe, rates Russia under

Putin a "six" with "seven" being the worst score. Similarly, Reporters without Borders, an international nongovernmental organization that promotes freedom of the press, places Russia under Putin in 147th place out of 165 evaluated nations.

As the Russian bear gains ground in Syria, continues murderous activities in Ukraine, and shows its teeth to the tiny Baltic nations, it is no wonder that senators like John McCain say we must stand up to Vladimir Putin. But, Dana Rohrabacher, the congressman who represents Laguna Beach and surrounding regions, amazingly takes the opposite position.

There are plenty of reasons for liberals to be at odds with Mr. Rohrabacher. He is against marriage equality and abortion rights, and at war with the science of climate change. But I hope that most conservatives would see his positions in regard to Putin, whom he once claimed to have arm wrestled, in the same light as respected Republicans John McCain and Lindsey Graham. Under Putin, Russia is a danger to the interests of our nation.

In 2014, Congress voted to offer aid to Ukraine and impose sanctions on Russia. The vote in the Senate was 98-2 in favor. In the House it was 399-19. Guess who was one of the 19? That's right, our very own Dana Rohrabacher. He has spoken of increasing political and social freedom in Russia, despite all the evidence to the contrary. Saying that we need to have better relations with Putin because he is fighting Islamic terrorism somehow creates a common cause. This ignores the far more dangerous game that Putin is playing in Syria, which, if successful, will prop up Assad and give the Russians a much stronger position in the Middle East. All at our expense.

Politico has referred to Congressman Rohrabacher as "Putin's top congressional ally." The *New York Times* says, "Dana Rohrabacher speaks up for Russia with pride." Even former Republican congressman Joe Scarborough, who hosts "Morning Joe," had to cut Rohrabacher's mic off during a contentious interview when the subject of Russian activities came up. When the segment was over, Scarborough lamented, "A little different from the Dana I served with."

Could it be possible that some brave Republican, who would like to make Putin a little less happy, could challenge Congressman Rohrabacher in the 2018 primary? He would have my vote.

James Utt is currently out of town. He is searching for the three to five million illegals that voted for Hillary Clinton. It could take some time.

TEACHING IN THE TIME OF TRUMP

"Do you miss teaching?" That question has been asked of me so many times since my retirement. I first stood in front of a classroom on trembling legs in 1969 at the age of 22. Too young, too inexperienced; enthusiasm would only carry me so far. My fellow teachers referred to me as "Mr. Green." But I grew into the job. Teaching became my career, my life, my love.

A dream haunts me at least once a week. It is Sunday night and I have no lesson plans for the next day. There will be chaos. My students will suffer. Then, through the fog of the dream state, comes the voice, "You're retired." A mixture of relief and sadness flows through me. Driving down Park Ave., similar feelings of relief and sadness arise as I navigate through the sea of minivan moms and SUV-clad dads near Thurston. Then, further down the hill, there is the high school, where there are young people looking not much different from those who sat in my classroom at El Toro High. This old teacher wonders if the fire and the desire to be that which he had been were still there.

During my years at El Toro, I taught a number of subjects, but by far my favorite was "Contemporary Issues," an elective class for juniors and seniors. The textbook was *Newsweek*, which was provided by the school. We would go through the articles together. I would provide background and pose questions pertaining to the issues. From time to time, we would leave *Newsweek* so I could introduce units on major controversies like the Arab-Israeli conflict, the death penalty, gay rights, gun control, and many others. I never expressed my own opinion on these issues, preferring to give the students both liberal and conservative arguments, and then challenging them to defend their positions. I tried my best to be a poor man's Socrates. Having been, over my long career, both a moderate conservative and a liberal, I could punch well with my "right" and my "left." Judging by letters of thanks from students stretching over thirty years, I must have done a pretty fair job at, well, being fair.

That would not be the case today. I could no longer teach my beloved "Contemporary Issues" class, because objectivity, so crucial to a teacher of social sciences, would be a near impossibility. I fear that I could not maintain any semblance of evenhandedness when it comes to the positions of our current president. Please keep in mind that I have voted for Republicans in past presidential elections, but President Trump is no George Herbert Walker Bush, Bob Dole, or John McCain. If you can find them, read a speech by Washington, Lincoln, or Reagan, and compare them to the tweets of President Trump, or his speeches before supporters when he ignores the teleprompter. The difference, as the president might say, is "Big League SAD."

According to our president, John McCain is not a war hero because he was captured. Take Iraq's oil, he says, which, according to conservative icon Charles Krauthammer, would be a war crime. Open admiration for the murderous Putin. These positions are disquieting in the extreme, but the most chilling is President Trump's attack on the mainstream media. In February he tweeted, "The Fake news media—failing NY Times, NBC News, ABC, CBS, CNN—is not my enemy. It is the enemy of the American people." I guess Fox News, with its evenhanded programming and guests like the thoughtful Ted Nugent, as well as Whitebart, I mean Breitbart News, is the great protector of the American people.

Newsweek, which I used for so many years in the classroom, stopped its print edition in January of 2013. There is a pretty good chance it would have fallen under the "fake news" category. The arbitrary division of news "helpful to the American people" and "the enemy of the American people" is greatly disturbing. Jonathan Karl of ABC—oh, I know, "fake news"—answers back, "A free press is not the enemy of America, it is a big part of what makes America great." Don't trust Karl because he is in the mainstream media? How about what John McCain said when he heard President Trump's remarks? "Dictators get started by suppressing free press."

So returning to the question, "Do I miss teaching?" the answer is yes, except for grading papers. But, maintaining an air of nonpartisanship would be very hard given the current administration. At this stage of my life better to be a columnist, free to express angst, joy, and whimsy.

James Utt hopes that this column will not cause President Trump to label the Laguna Beach Independent *as "Fake News."*

ARE WE BECOMING
MORE IGNORANT?

MAYBE WE DON'T see it in Laguna Beach. After all, look at us. Of residents over twenty-five, 97 percent have graduated from high school. 65 percent have at least a B.A., the highest percentage of any place in the area. Our outstanding schools, with their hardworking teachers, have standardized test scores that are high above the state and national average.

And yet, look outside our exquisite bubble and one sees disquieting signs, neon signs, flashing, and "warning ahead." Nearly three in ten Americans admit to having not read a book in the last year. This number has been on the uptick in recent years. More disturbing still is that only two in ten of us get our news from print newspapers. But wait, you say, I get good information from the Internet, social media, and late-night comedians. "I don't need books or print newspapers." Nothing could be more disheartening for an old teacher to hear. I am always in the middle of a book and become apoplectic if my morning paper is not delivered on time.

I recently ran across a book by Tom Nichols, a professor of national security affairs at the US Naval War College, entitled *The Death of Expertise*. He notes that there are one billion sites on the

Internet and observes, "The sheer size and volume of the Internet, and the inability to separate meaningful knowledge from random noise, means that good information will always be swamped by lousy data and weird detours."

Nichols quotes the columnist Frank Bruni who says, "Although the Internet could be making us smarter, it makes many of us stupider, because it's not just a magnet for the curious. It's a sinkhole for the gullible. It renders everyone an instant expert. You have a degree? Well, I did a Google search!"

Alexander Pope said, "A little knowledge is a dangerous thing." How much more dangerous if the "knowledge" is not knowledge at all, but rather a post by someone who has no real understanding of the subject. How much harm have Jenny McCarthy and Jim Carrey done with their unscientific anti-vaccine campaign? A campaign, I might add, that has gained popularity with some liberal communities.

Thanks to the Internet, people can seek out sites that reinforce their positions, living in a type of echo chamber. We want to confirm what we already believe. As Nichols points out, "Principled, informed arguments are a sign of intellectual health and vitality in a democracy." This cannot happen unless we have a citizenry that knows not only their own point of view, but also the arguments against their point of view. I used to tell my students that they could not really understand and defend their own position on an issue unless they were familiar with the strongest arguments against it. Thanks to the siren song of the Internet, people are less and less likely to seek arguments that go against their preconceived notions.

Look, I am an old dog, and Facebook is a relatively new trick, but still. Mark Zuckerberg, what hath you wrought upon the land? According to the *New York Times*, the average American spends between forty and fifty minutes a day on Facebook. This compares to just nineteen minutes a day that Americans spend reading. So much to learn, so little time, so many distractions. Wouldn't our country be better served if you had your face in a book, actually learning things from people who have some degree of expertise?

We are becoming more and more a nation where people think their knowledge is just as reliable as anyone else's. Usually, it is not. Let us remember the words of the late Senator Daniel Patrick Moynihan, "Everyone is entitled to his own opinion, but not his own facts."

Laguna, as I said, is an exception to this trend. But I must admit, as I take my morning walks, I see fewer and fewer newspapers on driveways.

James Utt would like to note that the women of the USA read more than the men do.

STUPIDITY, XENOPHOBIA, AND TRAGEDY

QUICK, NAME FIVE members of the Kardashian clan. Feel free to include spouses. I bet you did pretty well. Now, list the top five religions in the world. Unless you are like super Jeopardy champ Ken Jennings, or a professor of comparative religions, this question, no doubt, proved to be much more difficult.

America is the most religious country among the industrialized nations of the world. But, paradoxically, we have an embarrassing lack of knowledge about our dominant religion, Christianity.

For example, over 50 percent of Protestants do not know that Martin Luther started the Protestant Reformation. When the discussion turns to religions other than Christianity, the lack of knowledge is appalling. Perhaps, students tune out when foreign religions are being taught. Or, even more worrisome, they attend a school where comparative religions are not taught at all. "Don't want my child learning about any false gods!"

But, there are tremendously important reasons why we in the United States should know at least some of the tenets of the world's major faiths. This brings us back to the question of the top five religions in the world. They are Christianity, Islam, Hinduism,

Buddhism and, in fifth place with 27 million followers, Sikhism. Most Americans would be surprised to learn that there are about as many Sikhs living in this country as there are people in Wyoming. Our own state has tens of thousands of Sikh residents. Locally, there is a Sikh temple in nearby Santa Ana, and Sikhs live in Laguna Beach.

Sikhism began in the Punjab region of India. Major tenets of the faith are a belief in monotheism, reincarnation, and karma. The founders stressed the universal qualities of equality and brotherhood. Sikhs serve God by serving others and they see it as their duty to defend the oppressed. Sikh men do not cut their hair. Doing this, they believe, would be going against the perfection of God's creation. Their uncut hair is wrapped in a turban. Since hair is an integral part of the faith, beards are also prominent. These distinctive features, coupled with a somewhat darker complexion, have to their great misfortune caused Sikhs to become the target of hate crimes. Mistaken for Muslims, they have suffered indignities, assaults, and death.

It is heinous enough when law abiding Muslim-Americans are victims of hate crimes perpetrated by ignorant xenophobes. More is the tragedy when Sikhs are mistaken for Muslims and attacked, have their hair cut, or are simply shot to death.

Soon after 9/11, a man in Arizona told a waiter he was going to go out and shoot "some towel heads." He also said that all Arabs should be shot. He obviously did not know that "Arab" is not a religion, but an ethnicity, and that many Arabs are Christians. Balbir Singh Sodhi, a gas station owner and Sikh, was outside his business, turban proudly on his head. He was shot dead by this man.

In August of 2012, neo-Nazi Wade Page entered a Sikh temple in Wisconsin and murdered five men and one woman. In March of this year, two Sikh men were shot and one died. A recent *Los Angeles Times* article made reference to the "swelling ranks of Sikhs targeted, in many cases, after being mistaken for Muslims." The article also mentions that Sikh community leaders have noticed an uptick in attacks and harassment since the election of 2016. This is not hard to understand when we reflect on the overheated rhetoric coming from certain politicians.

A good friend and Laguna resident, Christine Fugate, a professor at Chapman's film school, went to London to film Sikhs for the Sikh Lens Program. She was there during the attack on London Bridge and Borough Market. When the police allowed citizens to lay flowers near where people had lost their lives, among the first to do so were Sikh Londoners.

Let me leave you with some words from Prabhjot Singh, a practicing doctor and professor at Columbia University. He and a friend were set upon and beaten by youths who were shouting, "Terrorist! Get Osama!"

As reported by CNN, Mr. Singh asked, "Why are we being attacked for being Sikh? My tradition teaches me to ask what are we doing as a community to have a far more welcoming embrace of people who are different from us?"

We all could learn a thing or two from the world's fifth largest religion.

James Utt hopes we can come to realize that the measure of a man is more than a turban and a beard.

TWO SHERIFFS

Last Saturday, two men came out to repair my garden fountain. They were on time, friendly, and very knowledgeable. They worked quickly, had the fountain up and running smoothly in no time, and explained how I was using the wrong chemicals in the war against algae.

They happen to have been Latinos and spoke with accents. Did the thought cross my mind, "Wonder if these guys have proper documentation?" Not for a second. They came, they smiled, they fixed. That was more than good enough for me.

Later that morning, I drove past the day laborer site in the canyon. This was the day after our Divider-in-Chief pardoned the former sheriff of Maricopa County, Joe Arpaio. I thought to myself how fortunate are these young men, as well as the fountain repairmen, that they were working in Laguna Beach, where our police force is led by someone like Chief Laura Farinella.

Fresh off her professional handling of the white identity group gathering on Main Beach, she stands as a symbol of so much that is good in our community. She is highly educated, a graduate of the FBI National Academy and FBI National Executive Institute, and has a long record of accomplishments from serving with the Long Beach police force. Chief Farinella believes in community based policing and working as a team. In her message to the residents of Laguna Beach on the police website, she says, "Law enforcement is a people business that is only successful through face-to-face community interaction and exchange of ideas." Given the fact that six million visitors pour into our city each year, it seems clear that the chief, and the men and women who work under her, are doing a great job of protecting and serving our city.

Then, there is Joe Arpaio. Before going into his law enforcement "techniques," let me mention a couple of things that should cause most people to seriously question his judgment. Spoiler alert: Liberal bias ahead. Sheriff Joe has said that President Trump will end up regarded as the greatest president in US history. Could someone please send him a biography of Abraham Lincoln? Or actually, a biography of almost any other president in our history. Even Millard Fillmore would do. After President Obama produced his long form birth certificate, Arpaio claimed it was a forgery. How could anyone believe ... oh, wait. According to an NBC poll, only 27 percent of Republicans agreed with the statement, "Barack Obama was born in the US." Look, I know Republicans. I play tennis with Republicans. They don't believe this canard. I'll bet Laguna Republicans are solidly in that 27 percent.

From 1993 to his well-deserved election defeat in 2016, Sheriff Joe reveled in being known as "America's toughest lawman." Probably most of us, even liberals like me, would not mind criminals being made a little uncomfortable during their stay with the authorities, but Sheriff Joe carried this to the extreme. He created a "Tent City" jail for the undocumented in the Arizona desert. In a speech, he once referred to it as a "concentration camp." Men housed there were given pink underwear and horrible food, and forced to endure temperatures that often rose to 115 degrees. Amnesty International described the place as inhumane, overcrowded, and dangerous. His department had to pay $142 million in settlements, legal fees, and compliance costs during his tenure.

Such things did not matter to the sheriff because he was

cracking down on "illegals." He ignored studies by the libertarian Cato Institute that reported, "undocumented immigrants do not commit a disproportional share of crime."

His men went on "sweeps" that detained people based solely on suspicion of their immigration status. These sweeps caused thousands of Latino residents to live in fear.

A federal judge concluded that he was using racial profiling, which flies in the face of the Fourth Amendment's protection against "unreasonable search and seizure." Simply put, the judge told him to knock it off. He disregarded this federal judge's ruling and continued to detain Latino residents. This earned him a criminal contempt conviction that could have put him behind bars for six months.

Wonder how he would have fared in the now destroyed "Tent City?"

But he will never be locked up in "the gray bar hotel," because fellow "birther," President Donald J. Trump, citing Arpaio's "years of admirable service to our nation," gave him a presidential pardon. I am aware that other presidents have given some pretty questionable people pardons in the past, but this one really rankles.

Chief Farinella, thanks for being the antithesis of Sheriff Joe.

James Utt notes that President Trump, besides wanting to build a wall, has put forward a proposal to significantly lower the number of legal immigrants allowed to enter the USA.

THE PERILS OF PARK AVENUE

I TRAVEL PARK Avenue to and from my home each day. It can be a perilous journey.

Sometimes I suffer just minor, but annoying, inconveniences that rankle, such as the super-slow driver plugging up the hill at 20 miles per hour, oblivious to the number of cars behind them. This week, it has been the repair crews reducing the road to one lane. But pokey drivers taking in the sights and necessary road repairs are things I am willing to endure. Other things not so much.

I live on the street right below Thurston Middle School, which seems to have a different starting time for certain days of the week. I really must learn this schedule. Every time I have a morning appointment in another city, there are the Thurston parents in minivan masses slowing things down to a crawl. When Thurston lets out a little after three, things get even worse. Some parents think it quite alright to park on corners, or make illegal U-turns if it helps them get in just the right position to make it easy for their kids to find them.

If I am extremely unlucky, I come up Park just as the high school is letting out. First, I come to the dreaded five-way stop where Park meets Legion, Short, and the parking lot exit. No one, I mean no one, waits his or her turn. Having negotiated this hazard, I come to a complete stop as the students casually jaywalk doing their best to look and act cool. I can't blame them. I was young once and tried to act cool, with very mixed results.

Finally comes summertime and there is no school traffic to block my advance. There are still plenty of things to put a driver in peril. There is the ridiculously narrow part of Park between St. Ann's and Skyline that tests my driving skills, as I navigate between parked cars and people that don't stay on their side of the road. Heaven help you if a large truck is coming the other way.

Those of you familiar with the area know there is a "yield" sign for the people coming down from Skyline as it merges onto Park. I don't know why so many people on Skyline take the "Yield" sign to mean "drive really fast and you can beat the people coming down Park."

Some years ago, there was a near tragic episode that happened on this small stretch of Park. Going up the street from St. Ann's, Park makes a jog to the left. Late one night a careless young driver did not make the jog and drove straight into a house, crashing into a bedroom that was thankfully empty at the time. When driving on that section of Park, please remember the words of Simon and Garfunkel, "Slow down, you move too fast."

I love to see the deer that roam Mystic Hills, but sometimes they decide to not look both ways before they cross Park Avenue. My late wife hit a deer, and not because she was speeding up the hill. She had just left the stop sign at Wendt when a deer bolted in front of her. Fortunately, it was a glancing blow and the young deer managed to disappear into the brush under his own power.

I have lived in Laguna long enough to know not to be overly critical of skateboarding, but I must relate this incident. Again, if you are familiar with Park, you know that just below Thurston there is a bend in the road, kind of a blind corner. Two large houses sit on the left as you go up the street. On trash day, the residents put their receptacles on the curb. The trash trucks must stop on Park to pick them up, pretty much blocking the entire lane. A young skater flying down from Top of the World made the turn at Tahiti and suddenly had to swerve into the left lane to avoid the trash truck. I was coming home and as I approached the bend suddenly there was a skateboarder in my lane. He had just enough time to get back into his lane. If I had been two or three seconds faster, he would not have had time to maneuver back to his lane. The chances are good he would be dead today.

Shaken by this, I decided to get to my home by taking the more circuitous route up Skyline. The first day I took this way, a young skater came barreling down the street in my lane. He fell off his board and it hit my car. Unhurt, he picked up the board and ran away. Why was it again that we didn't build a skateboard park around here?

Please drive with patience and caution when on Park. And parents, don't block my street or driveway when you pick your child up from Thurston.

James Utt swears he saw a chupacabra late one night at the corner of Park and Tahiti.

YOU CAN'T LOSE WHAT
YOU NEVER FOUND

THE STATE MOTTO of California is "Eureka," a Greek word meaning "I have found it." Many Americans believed they were experiencing a eureka moment when they watched Barack Obama give his victory speech in Grant Park on election night 2008. Strangers in the crowd hugged each other, tears rolled down the face of Jesse Jackson, chants of "Yes, we can" filled the air.

The United States of America had elected a black man to be its president.

Ours is a nation whose original sin was slavery, written down in the Constitution in black ink and light-colored parchment. America has been a nation of Jim Crow, the KKK, lynching, and of young black girls being blown apart in a Birmingham church. It is where Chaney, Goodman, and Schwerner were buried in shallow graves and Martin Luther King lay dead on a Memphis balcony. Even our paper currency has images of slave owners engraved on some bills. But now its Commander in Chief was a black man. All the work, marching, and education had changed hearts and minds. We thought we had come upon a time where we could speak of our nation as "post-racial." The sins of the past had been expunged.

But, we were wrong. Nine years after that exhilarating speech at Grant Park, we find America to be not that much different than the famous Kerner Commission description in 1969. That sobering report said, "Our nation is moving towards two societies: One white, one black—separate and unequal." The shining hopefulness we felt with the election of President Obama was nothing more than fool's gold. We had not found, nor created a post-racial America.

For a time, a brief time, the forces of racial animus retreated into the shadows, but the usual suspects soon emerged. Clown Prince Glenn Beck opined, "Obama has a deep-seated hatred for white people." While President Obama was addressing a joint session of Congress, South Carolina Congressman Joe Wilson shouted, "You lie!" Do you think he would have shown such disrespect for a white president? By the way, after this outburst, his support in his district increased and campaign contributions poured into his office.

Then came the "birther movement." Huge sections of the American public were all too eager to believe that this black man was not really a citizen of this country, but was actually born in Kenya and, on top of that, was actually a Muslim. According to an NBC poll only 27 percent of Republicans agree with the statement, "Barack Obama was born in the United States." The person that gave the most oxygen to this odious claim was a thrice-married television reality star and oft-sued real estate mogul, Donald Trump.

As the leader of the birther movement, he got lots of television time and his stature on the national stage increased. In 2015, he declared himself a candidate for the Republican nomination for president. What a joke, we liberals thought. His ridiculous charges against Obama's citizenship, his plan to build a wall to keep out Mexican rapists and drug dealers, his proposed Muslim ban would not catch on in a post-racial society. He would be swept into the dustbin of history.

Yet, his "Make America Great Again" slogan, which was a dog whistle for many who wanted to "Make America Whiter Again," began to give Trump traction. Millions of working-class whites rallied to his cause. They simply feared "the other," which they saw as a threat to their traditional values and to their tenuous grip on their position in American society.

To the astonishment of the political class, Trump earned the Republican nomination for president. To the crushing dismay of Democrats, he was elected president. Claiming he lost the popular vote only because illegals voted against him—there are those troublesome dark-skinned people again—he launched a campaign to root out voter fraud, which every previous study has shown to be virtually nonexistent. The Southern Poverty Law Center have noted a spike in the number of hate groups since the election of Donald Trump. Should we really be surprised by this? Remember after the violence in Charlottesville in August of 2017, President Trump said there were "good people" marching with the neo-Nazis and white supremacists. This earned the praise of David Duke, former leader of the KKK.

American racism did not disappear in 2008. It just retreated into the shadows waiting for a time to reemerge.

Post-racial America? If we were, would we still have statistics like the following: White poverty rate 9 percent, black poverty rate 24 percent, blacks six times more likely to be incarcerated, black men aged 19-34 nine times more likely to be shot by police than whites the same age. Ask yourself, how often is a white police officer found guilty for shooting an unarmed black person? How many black motorists are pulled over for the crime of "driving while black?" How many Americans are still judged by the color of their skin, rather than the content of their character?

Yes, we elected a black president and he was an outstanding father, husband, and leader. But his presidency brought to the surface the poison that is deep within the DNA of so many Americans. We have indeed come upon our eureka moment. We have found that we are, as we have always been, a racist nation.

James Utt hopes we will someday have a true eureka racial time.

FURRY HATS AND
SCULPTURE TRIOS

ON THE *LATE Show*, Stephen Colbert does a hilarious segment wearing a giant furry hat, reminding viewers that all-powerful rulers like Genghis Khan wore such lids. He proclaims that anything he says will now and forever become law. If I had a hat with such power, I would proclaim the following laws:

Let it be written that anyone who does not wait his turn at a four-way stop on Glenneyre Street is subject to a citizen's arrest. Their punishment will be to sit in the middle of the sculpture trio in front of the fire station for four hours. I know this comes close to violating the Eighth Amendment's "cruel and unusual punishment" clause. But, what the hell, they deserve it.

From this day forward when locals, who support restaurants year-round, are told there is a waiting list for a table, their names shall be placed before all tourists.

Henceforth, when anyone buys a house in town in order to tear it down and build a larger one, they must rent a house next door during construction. They, too, must share in the noise, dust, and parade of contractors that their future neighbors must endure.

I declare that from this day until the end of days, Fox News will appear on Comedy Central.

It is now and forever law that bicycle riders in our town can no longer pedal with that smug grin that says, "I own the moral high ground, because I have a smaller carbon footprint than you."

From now on, parking lots that charge exorbitant fees on weekends and holidays must wash and wax the cars that must pay to park there.

Again, let it be written that Birkenstocks, no matter what recent fashion magazines have said, are still ugly, and are banned within the city limits.

It is now and forever law that anyone wishing to run for city council must write an essay explaining what he really thinks of the sculpture group in front of the fire station.

Let it be known that anyone who pays by check at the supermarket and then does the subtraction in his bank book, thus holding up the line, is banned from that store for all of eternity.

Henceforth, there will be an age limit on males in Laguna Beach who wear baseball caps backwards. That age will be twelve.

From now on, those wishing to use the basketball courts on Main Beach, where once good players performed for appreciative crowds, must now pass a skills test before being allowed to fling their bricks toward the rim. They must be able to dribble and chew gum at the same time.

It is declared that millennials on a restaurant date who look at their cell phones more than once instead of engaging in conversation shall immediately be asked to leave and go to Newport Beach.

Any visitor to our art festivals who is heard saying, "*I* could paint that," should immediately be forced to paint that.

Let it be known throughout the city that the test of good citizenship is to fling one's self in front of the sculpture trio before a tourist can take a picture of it. We are a town known for its art. Let's not ruin our reputation. When faced with moral dilemmas, citizens of Laguna Beach must ask themselves, "What would Atticus do?"

While not a decree, the hat strongly recommends that all those passing on foot between Brooks and Cress streets stop at Laguna Beach Books. Local treasures are not to be missed.

I declare, from this day until the end of days, that each bartender in town must ask the following question: "Would you like that to be a double?"

The hat has spoken.

James Utt wears only a Los Angeles Angels cap, which sadly confers little power.

LAGUNA REFUSES
TO GO TO POT

IN 1996, CALIFORNIA legalized medical marijuana and a majority of Laguna Beach voters supported this initiative. In 2016, 57 percent of California voters supported Prop. 64, which legalized recreational marijuana. I would be very surprised if a majority of Laguna's electorate did not support this measure. Yet, the City Council and the voters have seen fit to allow no medical marijuana dispensaries in town and are making use of a provision in Prop. 64 that allows individual cities to ban recreational sale, as well.

Laguna is not alone in south Orange County when it comes to putting obstacles in the path of those that wish to buy a legal commodity. The "not in my backyard" attitude on this issue has taken root in several surrounding cities. I wish we would reconsider our position. My wife died an agonizing death due to cancer. Marijuana would have helped with the side effects of chemo as well as the increasing pain, as she came ever closer to death's doorstep. She chose the "medical martini" over medical marijuana. But, *if* she had wanted to use marijuana to ease her burden, driving two or three minutes to a medical dispensary here in town to speak with someone face-to-face about her options would have been a lot more convenient and humane than driving to Santa Ana.

The arguments put forward to defeat Measure KK are the same arguments the City Council is using to justify its banning of recreational sales. As Councilman Robert Zur Schmiede says, retail sales in our town "could attract loitering, criminal activity, and increased traffic."

To loiter is to "stand or wait around idly without apparent purpose." Councilman, I have loitered in the past and I will loiter in the future. Some of my greatest adventures began with me just loitering about. Great worry? I think not.

Increase in criminal activity? Many cities are using debatable data from Denver to make this claim. Denver police spokesman Sonny Jackson reports, "Crime is up, but I don't know if you can relate it to marijuana." According to the FBI Uniform Crime Report, marijuana crimes in Denver make up less than 1 percent of all offenses counted.

When it comes to cities most associated with marijuana use, one thinks of Amsterdam. According to the logic of our City Council, there should be rampant criminal activity there. Yet, the Safe Cities Index in 2015 rated Amsterdam the fifth safest city in the world.

Some of you are no doubt worried that selling marijuana will lead to greater use. However, the Cato Institute, founded by one of the Koch brothers, thus no wild-eyed liberal organization, issued a report on this subject. The report says, "Our conclusion is that state marijuana legalizations have had minimal effects on marijuana use and related outcomes."

In the trio of dangers listed by Robert Zur Schmiede—loitering, crime, traffic—let us notice that health concerns go unmentioned. There is good reason for this omission. A January 2015 article in *Scientific Reports* states that the mortality risks associated with marijuana use are 114 times less than with alcohol. Over 100,0000 people die each year from alcohol-related effects. Tobacco deaths total over 480,000. Remind me. Does Laguna allow the retail sale of these products?

Attorney General Jeff Sessions, no friend of states that have legalized marijuana, says its effect "is only slightly less awful" than heroin's. As reported in the *L.A. Times*, 13,000 people died from heroin overdoses in 2015, according to the Centers for Disease Control and Prevention. Guess how many Americans died from marijuana overdose? None. Sessions has also said "… good people don't smoke marijuana." Here is a partial list of past and current users who might come to our town and engage in criminal activities, or even worse, loitering: Former New York mayor Michael Bloomberg, Martha Stewart, Morgan Freeman, David Letterman, Colorado Governor John Hickenlooper, Dr. Sanjay Gupta, Phil Jackson, Maya Angelou, and two of the past three presidents. Oh, and Snoop Dogg, too.

A reminder to our City Council and their supporters on this issue: *Reefer Madness* was not a Ken Burns documentary. It is possible to have well-regulated retail marijuana outlets as the law proscribes, without turning Laguna Beach into San Francisco's "Summer of Love."

James Utt forgot to mention that Congressman Dana Rohrabacher favors legalized medical marijuana. Even a stopped clock is right twice a day.

TIME TO TAKE OFF
OUR UNIFORMS

THERE ARE THOSE that think that columnists for local papers should stick to writing about local issues. This writer usually does. Pot sales in town, our city's gay heritage, our magnificent local bookstore, how Laguna is, well, not Newport Beach. All have been touched on over the years. But for this column, a broader issue will be addressed.

The voices of women who have brought credible accusations of sexual assault and harassment have risen to a crescendo across this nation. Let us count but a few of those fired, disgraced, or forced into exile: Charlie Rose, Louis CK, Roger Ailes, Bill O'Reilly, Harvey Weinstein. Yet, there is one arena where women's accusations seem to take a back seat to more "important" considerations, and that is in the political arena.

Governor Kay Ivey of Alabama says she believes the women who have come forward alleging that Roy Moore engaged in sexual misconduct, including child molestation, with a 14-year-old. Yet, she intends to vote for him because it is better to have a Republican in office than a Democrat. Unfortunately, this is not an isolated view. Our president and many others have said basically the same thing.

It seems many Americans wear uniforms that both have an "R"

or a "D," and for them political considerations override anything else. Need an insuring vote to see that a tax bill gets through? Then by all means, let's allow an accused pedophile into the most august legislative body in the world.

A few brave Republicans, like Mitch McConnell and Paul Ryan, have taken a strong stand against Moore as has the president's own daughter. When one reads the story in the *Washington Post* with all its corroborating evidence, then listens to Judge Moore's stammering self-defense on Sean Hannity's show, it is difficult to believe his denials. There needs to be a communal consensus that we will put morality above political expediency. This must be done before our political uniforms sink so deeply into our skin that we become nothing more than warring tribes where political compromise, even civil discourse, is impossible.

Lest some of you think this is little more than a liberal hit piece against a good man from Alabama, let me be clear about a couple of things. Given the number of women who have come forward with accusations against Senator Al Franken, one with a picture of him groping her while she slept on a flight home from a USO tour, I believe he should step down immediately, even if the level of his transgression does not rise to the level of Moore's. Is it too much to ask that the members of our Senate be of the highest moral quality?

For many liberals, this time of women coming forward with their stories should cause a painful reexamination of President Bill Clinton. Not just his relations with Monica Lewinsky, which at the time was dismissed by most feminists as just "consensual sex." It was certainly not worthy of impeachment, they said. One female reporter said she would perform the same act on Clinton as a way of giving thanks for keeping abortion legal. Looking at this tawdry episode today, I hope that most of us see it for what that was—a powerful man getting sex because he was powerful. Impeach, probably not; resign, I would hope so.

What about those other women who claimed sexual abuse at the hands of President Clinton? Paula Jones, Juanita Broaddrick,

Kathleen Willey. Would we liberals be so quick to dismiss their claims today? I would hope not. The Clinton camp trashed them at the time. Top advisor James Carville said of Jones, "Drag a hundred dollar bill through a trailer park, you never know what you'll find." What would be the reaction if such a statement was made today? Let us hope it would be met with the same contempt it should have been met with in the 1990s.

Some commentators are saying we have reached a tipping point. Women will not be afraid to come forward when they have been sexually mistreated. For this to happen, we men must come to grips with the fact that for eons, women have been mistreated. We must not tolerate those who have done so. In the Old Testament, women were little more than property. In the 1960s, the Rolling Stones felt it cool to sing about their girlfriend as being "Under My Thumb." Now women are speaking out. Let us listen to their voices.

Powerful figures in the entertainment industry and the press have gotten the punishment they deserve. I hope when it comes to politics, we will not let our uniforms stand in the way of decency.

James Utt reminds us that over a dozen women have charged President Trump with inappropriate sexual behavior. He has said he will sue them all. So far, he has not filed one suit.

BIO

James Utt is a fifth-generation Orange Countian who has witnessed dramatic changes in his 70 years. He served in the United States Army, taught high school for 37 years, and now watches the world spin by from his home in Laguna Beach. Currently his columns appear in the *Laguna Beach Independent*. He has had his work published in the *Sun* and *Lit Central Orange County*.

He plays tennis, and wishes he had a more consistent serve.

ACKNOWLEDGEMENTS

YOU WOULD NOT be holding this book in your hands if it were not for Christine Fugate, a filmmaker, writer, and teacher at Chapman University, my alma mater. Friend, mentor, sister from another mother, she convinced me—nagged me?—into believing I could write things people would actually like to read.

Andrea Adelson, editor of the *Laguna Beach Independent*, appreciated my work enough to make me a regular columnist. For this, I am eternally grateful.

I would also like to thank my sons, Bryan and Steven, for their past and present inspiration and encouragement, as well as my late wife whose memory shapes many of my writings.

There is also my sister who helps me see that cats can be terrible creatures. Thank you also to her husband, John, my doubles partner. I have let him down so many times on the court that if I am found dead, the police should start their investigation with him.

I am indebted to Stephen Colbert for the Big Furry Hat, and for showing that at least one good thing can come out of South Carolina.

Finally, special thanks to Sharon Dickson, who kept me from going over the edge. Several times.

Made in the USA
Columbia, SC
02 May 2018